Material appearing on pages 8–13 and 34–61
copyright © Grisewood & Dempsey Limited 1976
as *Ward Lock's Children's Encyclopedia*

Material appearing on pages 14–33 and 62–89
copyright © Grisewood & Dempsey Limited 1977
as *Ward Lock's Children's Encyclopedia of Science*

Cover © Rand McNally & Company 1982

Printed in the United States of America by Rand McNally & Company
Library of Congress Catalog Card No. 82-80678

First printing, 1982

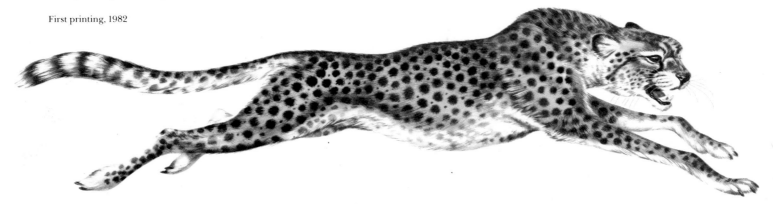

Rand McNally's

Children's Encyclopedia of SCIENCE

Edited by John Paton

Rand McNally & Company
Chicago / New York / San Francisco

Contents

ABOUT THIS BOOK

Science plays a major role in nearly every part of modern life. The mysteries of the universe can be seen through a telescope. The excitement of a space flight can be watched on television. And from opposite sides of the globe, people can speak to each other simply by dialing a telephone.

Rand McNally's Children's Encyclopedia of Science explains the basic scientific principles behind many of these natural and technical "mysteries." What causes a rainbow, why the sky is blue, how a television works, and how a record is made are a few of the topics covered. The contributions of some of our greatest inventors and scientists are told. And throughout the book and in the Fun with Science section, simple, safe experiments that require no special equipment prove the ideas set forth. On the last three pages, an index is included for easy reference to subjects of interest.

Rand McNally's Children's Encyclopedia of Science is an important book for anyone curious about the wonders of our world.

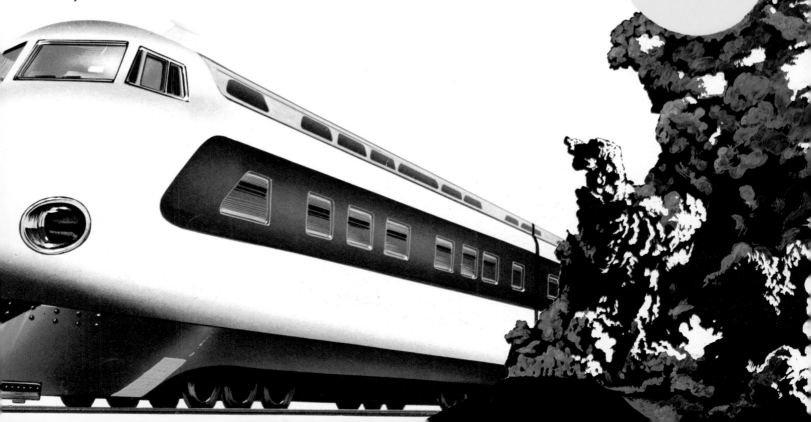

Our Earth in Space

The earth is only a tiny speck among all the stars and planets. But it is our home and just right for us to live on.

Our earth seems very big to us, but it is just one of nine planets that move around the sun. The sun and everything that spins around it make up the 'Solar System'.

This is the earth as a spaceman sees it.

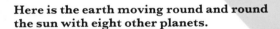

Here is the earth moving round and round the sun with eight other planets.

A Lot of Suns

A famous astronomer once said that there are more stars like our sun in the universe than there are grains of sand on all the beaches in the world. Yet all these stars are very far apart. Our own sun has lots of room to move about in. Its nearest star neighbor is 25,000 million miles away. It has been said that if there were only three kangaroos in Australia the country would be more crowded with kangaroos than space is with stars.

Our sun is much bigger than all its planets put together. It is also very, very hot. But our sun is just a star – a very ordinary star. It is two-thirds of the way from the center of a whole cluster of stars called a 'galaxy'. At night we can see it as the Milky Way.

On the right is our vast galaxy of stars. The sun and its planets are the speck of light at the point of the arrow. But there are millions of galaxies. Our whole huge galaxy is only a speck among them (below).

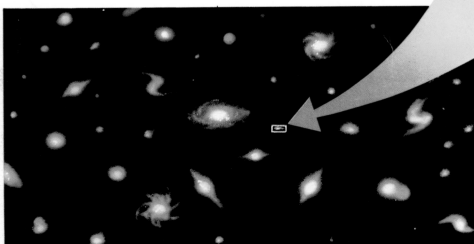

But this galaxy of stars – our galaxy – is only one of millions of galaxies. Some of these galaxies are so far away the light from them has taken over 5,000 million years to reach us.

All this shows how small our earth is in the vast universe. But to man it is a perfect home. It is the only planet in the Solar System with the right temperature and atmosphere to allow men to live.

Among the millions of unseen planets out in space there must be others with conditions like the earth's. On these planets there must be beings who may, one day, get a message through to us.

The picture above is a small part of the Bayeux Tapestry. The tapestry was embroidered on a strip of linen 76 yards long and shows the conquest of England by the Normans in 1066. This piece shows people pointing in astonishment at Halley's Comet. The picture on the right shows what the comet looked like when it last appeared in 1910.

What are Stars?

The stars we see in the night sky are like our sun. But they look small because they are very far away. Some are smaller than our sun. Others are hundreds of times bigger.

The stars seem to move across the sky. But it is the earth that is moving. The earth spins like a top. It also travels around the sun.

Scientists think that stars are made from clouds of gas and dust. A star begins to shine when atomic explosions start inside it, making it very hot. Our sun shines because there are always vast numbers of huge explosions, just like hydrogen bomb explosions, going on inside it.

Comets and Shooting Stars

Comets are big balls of dust and gas that travel through space. They travel round the sun, just like the planets. As you can see from the picture above, they have long glowing tails. This is Halley's Comet which can be seen from earth every 76 years. It was last seen in 1910 and will be seen again in 1986.

Meteors are pieces of rock that journey round the sun. We cannot see them until they enter the earth's blanket of air. Then they glow white hot as they streak through the night sky. They are also called 'shooting stars'.

Meteors usually burn up before they reach the ground. But sometimes big ones do hit the earth.

Huge radio telescopes like the ones on the right receive signals sent out by stars too far away to be seen by ordinary telescopes. They are also used to track spacecraft.

Our Neighbor the Moon

The moon is our nearest neighbor in space. It is only 240,000 miles away, which is quite close when we think that the sun is nearly 400 times further away.

We Only See One Face

We can call the moon 'our moon' because it really does belong to us. It is a *satellite* of our earth and makes a complete circle round us in a month. The moon itself is also spinning. It takes it a month to make one spin. This means that we always see the same face of the moon from earth. It was only when we were able to send spacecraft round the moon that we found out what the back of our neighbor was like. And it was found that the back is very much like the face we see from earth.

Moonlight is Really Sunlight

When we look at the full moon on a clear night we are often surprised how brightly it shines. But the moon is not giving out any light at all. All it is doing is reflecting light from the sun.

The picture below shows what happens. Sunshine is coming in from the left. It hits one side of the earth and one side of the moon. Standing on the dark side of earth we can look up and see the sunlight shining on the moon.

How Big is the Moon?

Very few people can guess how big the moon is. Because we see it in the sky looking as big as the sun, we think it is bigger than it really is. The moon is not very big. In fact, it is almost exactly the same size as Australia, as you can see in the picture above.

The moon is so small it cannot hold an atmosphere around it as the earth does. There is no air to breathe on the moon, so spacemen have to take their own air with them.

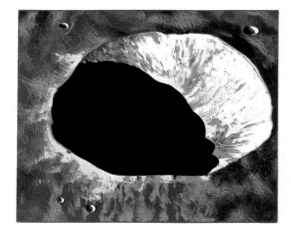

The Strange Craters

It has been known for hundreds of years that the moon's surface is covered with strange circles. These are called *craters*, and some of them are 186 miles across. The picture above shows one close up. It is thought that the craters have been caused by volcanoes.

The Moon's Eclipse

The earth travels round the sun and the moon travels round the earth. Sometimes the sun, the earth and the moon come in line with each other. Then the moon is eclipsed by the earth's shadow. You can see this in the picture below. The sun's light is coming in from the right. The light cannot reach the moon because the earth is in the way.

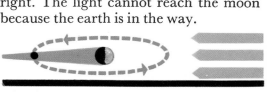

The picture on the left shows the moon as you would see it through a large telescope. You can see the craters. And there are also big dark areas. People used to think these dark areas were seas on the moon. They gave them names like 'Sea of Rains' and 'Ocean of Storms'. But now we know that there are no seas on the moon. The dark areas are just dry, flat plains. The moon has no water. It is a dry, lifeless place. There is no rain, no wind, no clouds, no weather.

Moon soil collected by the spacemen was made up of tiny pieces of rock and glass.

It is thought that many small craters on the moon have been made by meteors.

Men on the Moon

Men first stepped on to the moon in the year 1969. They were doing something very strange – something no man had ever done before.

Why was stepping on the moon so strange? First of all, there was no air there. The spacemen had to carry their own air in containers on their backs. And because there was no air, the spacemen couldn't speak to each other, no matter how loudly they shouted through their helmets. Sound needs air to travel through. They had to speak to each other by radio.

And the spacemen had to be very careful how they walked. Because the moon is so small, things on its surface weigh only a sixth of what they do on earth. And this includes spacemen.

A Very Hot World

The spacemen had also to wear specially cooled suits. Without them they would have burned up in the fierce heat on the moon's surface. Because there is no atmosphere on the moon, the sun's rays beat down with nothing to stop them. The temperature can rise to over 248°F.

The picture above shows the spacemen landing on the moon, with the earth shining down out of a black sky. On the left is the *Lunar Rover* which later spacemen used to drive about the moon.

The picture on the right shows spaceman Neil Armstrong. He was the first man to step on to the moon's dusty surface.

11

The Air Around Us

The earth is covered by a blanket of air which stretches upwards for a few hundred miles. Without this 'blanket' there would be no living creatures on earth. Our planet would be a barren world like the moon, boiling hot all day and freezing cold each night.

The Air is Vital

Without air we could not breathe. But air is vital to us in other ways. It helps shield us from dangerous rays that come in from outer space. Like a blanket, it keeps the earth warm at night and shields us from the sun's fierce heat during the day.

The air also allows us to hear things. Sound waves travel in the air. Without air we would have to talk to each other by radio, as astronauts have to do on the moon.

Our blanket of air is also called the *atmosphere*.

Air and No Air

If you look at the pictures on these pages you will see how small a distance above and below the earth's surface we move in. Imagine that the top of this page is about 100 miles above sea level. There is hardly any air up there. The mountain below is Everest, the highest in the world. Birds cannot fly as high as Everest.

The big Jumbo jet plane is flying at 33,000 feet. The fast-flying Concorde is flying at 56,000 feet. There is not enough air for people to breathe at the height these planes fly at. So the planes have to take their own air supply with them.

The dark blue area below shows the deepest part of the sea – 36,000 feet below sea level.

Air Has Weight

Air can be weighed. If you weigh an 'empty' bottle, you are weighing both the bottle and the air inside it. Pump the air out of the bottle and weigh it again. It will be lighter. The difference between the first and second weight is the weight of the air that was in the bottle.

On the right you can see the earth, surrounded by its blanket of air. The air gets thinner and thinner the higher one goes. At a height of 300 miles there is hardly any air at all.

Air presses on everything. To show this, take a glass of water and place a card over the top (left). Turn the glass upside down (center). When you take your hand away (right) the card stays in place. This shows that the air pressure beneath is greater than the weight of the water.

High on Mount Everest the air is so thin, men have to wear oxygen masks.

The Air Above Us

Our earth is unlike other planets in the sun's system in many ways. But perhaps the most important difference is that it is surrounded by air. Compared to the size of the earth, this layer of air is not very thick. It goes upwards from the earth's surface for only a few hundred miles. And about half of all the earth's air is pulled into the 5 miles closest to the surface. Above this the air is so thin, men cannot move about easily without wearing oxygen masks.

At a height of 300 miles there is hardly any air at all.

Why is the Sky Blue?

The sky is blue because the sun's light has to shine through our atmosphere. Sunlight is a mixture of light of all colors. Our atmosphere is made up of air, dust, and tiny particles of water. As sunlight passes through, its blue light is scattered more than its other colors. This scattered light we see as blue sky.

Floating on Air

The hovercraft above is floating on a cushion of air. In fact, hovercraft are often called air cushion vehicles. They are something between a ship and a plane. Powerful jet engines push air downwards through the bottom of the craft. This air lifts the craft off the water. It can then skim over the surface of the waves very quickly, pushed by propellers like a plane. It can also travel over land.

The hovercraft above is carrying cars and people at 62 miles per hour between England and France.

Rubbing Against Air

When anything rubs against anything else there is what we call *friction*. Friction makes things hot. Rub your hands together hard. They get hot. When you rub a match against a matchbox, so much heat is made the match bursts into flame.

When things go through air they get hot too. Fast planes have to be made of special metal that doesn't melt from the heat. When spacemen come back to earth in their space capsule (above) they whizz through our air at a terrific speed. The front of the space capsule has to be made of a very special material that burns away slowly in the great heat caused by the air.

The highest layer of the atmosphere is called the 'ionosphere'. Beyond it lies empty space. In the ionosphere the atoms in the air are electrified by streams of particles coming in from space. These electrified atoms are very useful to us. They reflect radio waves back to earth a long way away. So we can send radio waves round the earth by bouncing them off the ionosphere.

We think of clouds being very high in the sky. But very few of them are as high as Mount Everest. The highest clouds are the streaky cirrus, and these are not found very often above 49,000 feet.

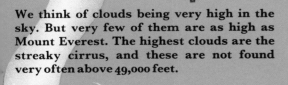

The highest a man has flown is about 22 miles. Helicopters can fly as high as 32,000 feet (right).

Man first rose off the ground because hot air rises. In 1783 the Montgolfier brothers in France filled a cloth bag with hot air. It rose several thousand feet into the air with two men aboard (left).

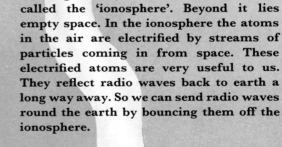

Water

Water is all around us and inside us. Without it there would be no life on earth. Water looks and tastes rather dull, but it is by far the most important liquid there is. It makes up nearly three-quarters of our weight. And a man must take in 2 or 3 quarts of it every day in food and drink.

Nearly three-quarters of the earth's surface is covered by water. Most of the fresh water on earth is frozen solid around the North and South Poles. Think how much fresh water there must be in the great Antarctic continent. The ice there is sometimes almost 2 miles thick.

We are all about three-quarters water. If we don't have any of it in food or drink for a week, we die.

Ripe watermelons are about 97 percent water.

A tomato is 95 percent water.

Even an egg is 74 percent water.

Water is Powerful

For thousands of years people looked at the power of waterfalls. Then someone thought of the water wheel — you can see one on the right. The fast-running water in the stream moved the paddles and turned the wheel. The wheel often turned a millstone to grind corn.

But the water wheel did not give much power. Its place was taken by the water turbine. Now great dams are built. The water from them is made to fall through huge pipes and hit the blades of the water turbine. This turns very fast and drives a generator to make electricity.

Frozen Water Floats

Water is also a strange liquid. It is one of the very few things that grows bigger (expands) when it freezes. That is why huge icebergs float. Icebergs are frozen fresh water.

The Strength of Water

What happens if we fill a bottle with water, stopper it tightly and put it in a freezer? The bottle bursts. This is because the water has grown bigger when it turned into ice. Water is very powerful stuff when it freezes. It can burst pipes. If it freezes in cracks in rocks it can split the rocks asunder.

The enormous power of waterfalls can be used to drive water turbines. Turbines turn electricity generators.

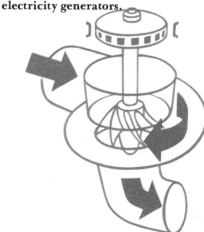

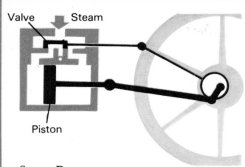

Valve Steam

Piston

This is *Puffing Billy,* one of the oldest steam engines. It was built in 1813 and can still be seen in the Science Museum in London. The invention of the steam engine started the modern Machine Age. Men could get all the power they wanted, just by heating water.

Steam Power

Water is also very powerful when it is heated and becomes a gas — steam. When water becomes steam it expands to about 1700 times its size. Steam engines use the energy of expanding steam to drive wheels or do other work. The diagram above shows how a simple steam engine works. A valve slides back and forward. It lets steam into the cylinder at one end, then at the other end. So the steam pushes the piston one way, then the other. The piston turns the wheel.

Water sticks to almost anything. If a narrow glass tube is dipped in water, the water rises some way up the tube. This is called *capillary action.* It is caused by the attraction between the water and whatever it touches. Water can rise up slowly through the walls of a house for the same reason (below). We call this 'damp'.

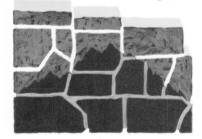

Water Facts

The oceans hold 97 percent of all the earth's water.

In one cubic mile of sea water there are 129,000,000 tons of table salt. In all the oceans there is enough salt to cover the continents with a layer 490 feet thick.

The jellyfish holds the animal record for the water inside it. This slithery creature is 95 percent water, almost the same as the sea water in which it lives.

Sea water is heavier than fresh water because of the salts dissolved in it.

Ordinary bread, even after baking in a hot oven, is still about one-third water.

Water Has a Skin

Place a dry needle on a piece of paper tissue. Float the paper carefully on some water. When the paper sinks the needle stays on the surface of the water. This shows that water has a sort of skin on its surface. If the needle breaks the skin it will sink.

The water strider below is an insect that actually walks on water. You can see the dents made by the insect's legs on the water's skin.

More than 20,000 kinds of fish live in the earth's oceans and rivers. Like land animals, they need oxygen to live. But they take their oxygen from the water instead of from the air as we do. Water goes in through the fish's mouth and passes over tiny blood vessels in the *gills.* Oxygen in the water is taken into the blood. Then the water goes out again through the fish's gill covers (below). Out of water a fish dies because it does not have lungs for air breathing.

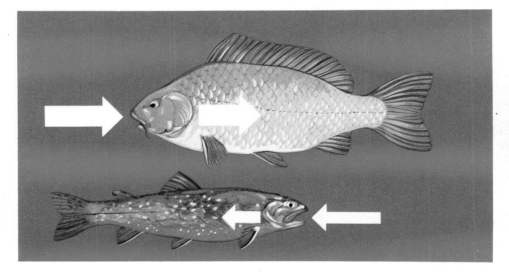

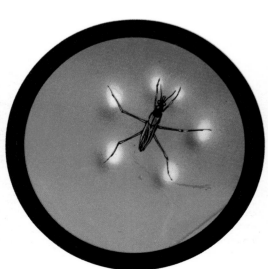

Light and Color

What is light — that strange stuff that comes in all colors from light bulbs, television sets, and fires? We are still not quite sure what it is. But we do know that most of our light comes from the sun. And the sun is very hot. When things are hot enough they give out light rays. Nearly everything that gives out light is hot.

Light waves travel very, very fast. Scientists believe that nothing can travel faster than light waves. They move at the same speed as radio waves and heat rays.

Breaking up White Light

The first man to find out about light was the great scientist Isaac Newton. He shone a beam of sunlight through a piece of glass called a *prism*. (You can see some prisms below.) The light that came out of the prism was broken up into all the colors of the rainbow — red, orange, yellow, green, blue and violet. Newton had found out that ordinary white light is made up of many colors added together.

The Rainbow's Colors

When sunlight falls on rain or spray, we sometimes see a rainbow. Rainbows are caused by the drops of water behaving like tiny prisms. They break up the sun's light into colors. Those colors are always in the same order, from red to violet.

Nature's Prisms

Many natural crystals, like those above, behave like prisms. They are able to break up white light into the colors of the rainbow.

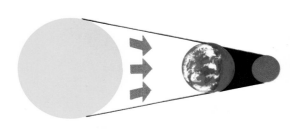

Moonshine

The moon has no light of its own. It only reflects light from the sun. We can see that this is so when the earth comes between the sun and the moon. The moon no longer shines. It is *eclipsed*.

What Makes a Light Bulb Shine?

When we switch on a light, electricity flows through a coil of special metal in the light bulb. This metal gets hot at once and gives out a bright white light.

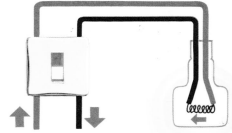

Many Colors Make White

You can show that many colors added together make white. Make a circle of cardboard with the colors as shown below. Spin the circle quickly and the cardboard looks almost white. When you look at white light you are seeing a mixture of colors.

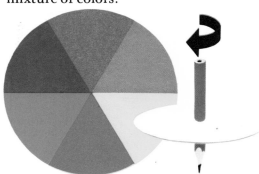

Making Things Bigger

A magnifying glass is thicker in the middle than at the edges. Light bounces off the pin and goes through the glass. The glass spreads the light before it reaches your eyes. The pin looks bigger.

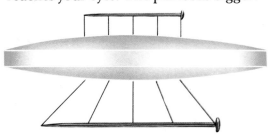

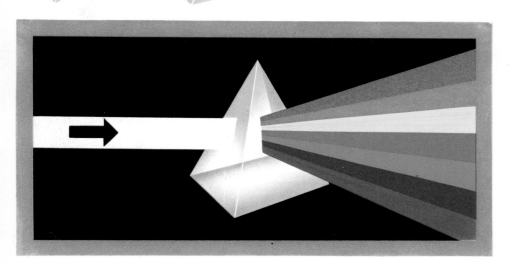

Mixing Colored Lights

As you can see in the picture on the left, red, green and blue lights can be mixed to make any other color. Red and green light mixed give us yellow light. If we add blue to the yellow light, we have white light. All the colors you see in a color television set are made up from these three *primary* light colors — red, green and blue.

Mixing Paints

If you ask an artist to name the three primary colors he will say yellow, blue and red. Mixing paints is quite different from mixing colored lights. If you mix yellow and blue paint you get green. But if you mix yellow and blue light you get white light, as we have seen above. You can make any color of paint you want by using yellow, blue and red paints. But you cannot make white paint, no matter how many colors you mix.

Why is a Red Flower Red?

A red flower is red because it takes in all the other colors and throws back only red. (See the picture on the right.) The black center of the flower takes in all the colors and gives none out. We see it as black. A white flower gives back to our eyes all the colors of light. We know that all the colors added together make white.

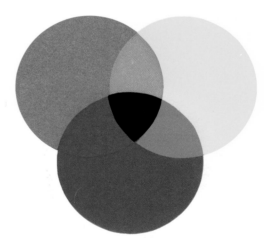

Using Light and Color to Survive

Some animals use light and color to hide themselves from their enemies.

The zebra's stripes make it difficult to see in its home grasslands.

The moth above produced black moths to hide against smoke-blackened trees.

Creatures that Make Light

Some creatures make their own light. Glow-worms and fireflies give out light to attract a mate. The deep sea angler fish (below) has a fishing rod dangling ahead of its mouth. A light twinkles at the end of the rod. Other fish are attracted to the light and are at once snapped up by the angler.

Hot and Cold

What is heat? On a summer day the heat can soften the tar on a road. Yet this is not even close to the temperature of boiling water. The temperature of molten steel (2732°F) is hotter still. Yet blast furnaces are chilly places indeed compared to the sun. On the sun temperatures soar to over one million degrees. Other stars are hotter still. There is no limit to how hot it can get.

Cold is a different matter. At 32°F water freezes into ice. The coldest place on Earth is a chilly −126°F. But the thermometer would have to drop to −297°F before the air started to freeze. At −459°F, absolute zero is reached. The temperature can go no lower. Here, everything is frozen solid. Nothing moves. Even the tiny atoms are locked in an icy grip.

As temperatures rise, atoms begin moving again. Their heat increases as they speed up. Since heat is a form of energy, their energy also increases. The more heat energy there is, the faster atoms whizz about. The faster they move, the higher the temperature rises.

The most important sources of heat, apart from the sun, are wood, coal, gas and oil. They all give off heat when they burn.

Heat From the Atom
In atomic power stations, the energy of the tiny atom is used to make electricity. Special radio-active fuel lies in the core of a reactor. By pushing control rods in and out the amount of heat produced is carefully controlled.

Measuring Hot and Cold
We measure the hotness or coldness of things with a *thermometer*. A thermometer measures hotness or coldness in *degrees*. The more degrees the hotter a thing is.

The small bulb at the end of a thermometer is filled with alcohol or mercury. As the alcohol or mercury is heated, it expands up a narrow column. Markings on the column tell us the number of degrees.

Heat From Friction
Heat is formed when things are rubbed together. If they are very smooth, not much heat is made. When the objects are rough, the amount of heat produced is greater. It may be enough to start a fire. This is how matches are lit.

Heat From Electricity
When electricity flows through metal, the metal atoms become 'excited'. They move about faster and give off much heat. This is how electric heaters and toasters work.

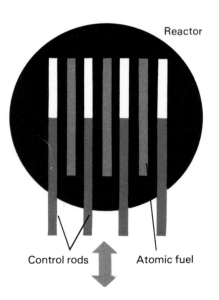

Reactor

Control rods   Atomic fuel

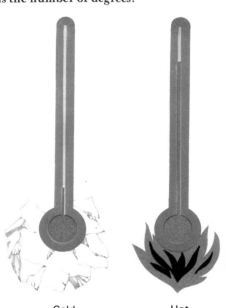

Cold   Hot

Power From the Sun
It is quite easy to set fire to paper on a sunny day. A magnifying glass does the job. It focuses the sun's rays. The paper soon begins to smoke. *Solar furnaces* like the one above capture the sun's heat in the same way. Huge mirrors direct the sunlight into a single point. Temperatures up to 6600° Fahrenheit are reached. This is hot enough to melt steel.

Keeping Heat In
Heat flows from hot to cold. *Insulation* stops this flow. A Thermos bottle keeps coffee hot all day. Insulation material in the walls of houses also keeps the heat inside. In the same way, an insulating jacket keeps hot water tanks from cooling too rapidly.

Heat From the Earth
The earth's center is red hot. Beneath the thin crust under our feet the heat is so great that even the rocks melt. Yet the furnace within the earth can be tamed. Geysers and hot springs can be tapped. Their steam is used to drive the turbines that turn electricity generators, and to heat homes as well.

Heat Changes Things
Most things change when they are heated. They grow larger in size — they *expand.* A pot full to the brim with water will overflow when the water gets hot. Things become smaller when they cool down — they *contract.*

Heat and cold also change the shape of things. If you take a lump of ice out of the refrigerator it will melt as it warms up. The atoms inside the ice move faster as they turn to water.

If we now put the water from the ice into a pot and heat it, the atoms in the water leap about very quickly. The water boils and turns into steam. If we boil the water for long enough it will all vanish as steam. Steam is a gas.

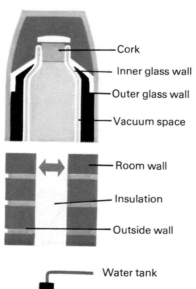

Cork
Inner glass wall
Outer glass wall
Vacuum space

Room wall
Insulation
Outside wall

Water tank
Insulating jacket
Heat control

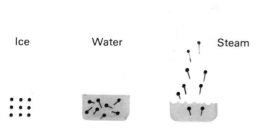

Ice　　　Water　　　Steam

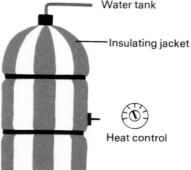

All things melt and boil at different temperatures. Ice melts at 32° Fahrenheit. Water boils at 212° Fahrenheit. The hotness or coldness of things is called their *temperature.*

Heat Makes Cold
A refrigerator can warm a room. This is because it is only cold on the inside. Place your hand outside around the back. You will find that it is warm.

A refrigerator has a special liquid that is first turned into vapor. This makes it take up heat from inside the refrigerator. The vapor is then compressed (squeezed). This changes it

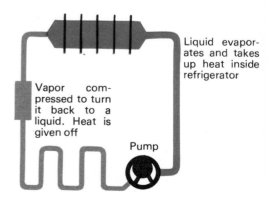

Liquid evaporates and takes up heat inside refrigerator

Vapor compressed to turn it back to a liquid. Heat is given off

Pump

back to a liquid. The liquid is pumped through a long, bent tube at the back of the refrigerator. There the liquid gives out the heat taken from inside the refrigerator. So the liquid and gas is pumped round and round. As the cycle continues, the refrigerator becomes colder inside and the air outside is warmed.

Sounds

The air is full of sounds — some pleasant, like the tinkle of a small bell, others unpleasant, like the noise of a door banging. But whether sounds are pleasant or unpleasant, they are all made by something moving. Before our ears can pick up a sound, something has to move in the air and make the air *vibrate*. These invisible vibrations travel through the air, and are called *sound waves*. Sound waves move through the air quite quickly — at about 1,115 feet a second. But they do not travel nearly as fast as light waves or radio waves.

Sounds Need a Carrier

If there were no air we could stand in a busy street and hear nothing. Sound waves need something to travel through. Light and radio waves do not need air. We can see light coming from the moon. We can speak by radio to spacemen on the moon. Yet these light and radio waves have traveled through space where there is no air. But no matter how loud a sound there was on the moon, we could not hear it, because there is no air.

What is Sound?

Sound is made by very fast back-and-forth movements called vibrations. Hold a ruler on a table so that it sticks out about 8 inches. When you pull up on the end of the ruler and let it go, the ruler vibrates in the air. Our ears pick up the sound waves made by the vibrating ruler. Now hold the ruler so that it sticks out about 6 inches and pull it down. The ruler vibrates faster this time. There are

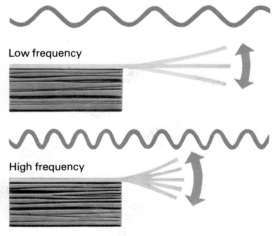

Low frequency

High frequency

more sound waves every second. Our ears hear a higher sound. We call the number of sound waves a second the *frequency* of the waves. The higher the frequency, the higher the sound we hear.

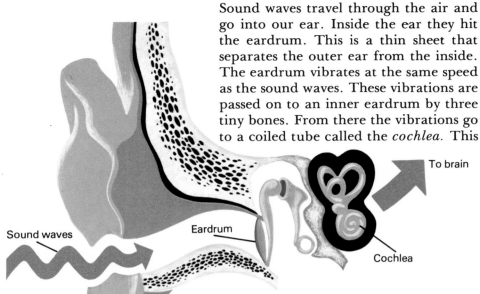

Bells and Gongs

Bells can be made of almost anything — clay, glass or even wood. But big bells are usually made of bronze — a mixture of copper and tin. They are cast in one piece and when struck vibrate to make a musical note.

The world's largest bell is in the Kremlin in Moscow. It weighs 196 tons but it broke before it could be rung.

Gongs have been used in the East for hundreds of years. They are made of metal and struck with a soft-headed hammer. When struck they vibrate with a loud 'boom'.

Our Wonderful Ears

Sound waves travel through the air and go into our ear. Inside the ear they hit the eardrum. This is a thin sheet that separates the outer ear from the inside. The eardrum vibrates at the same speed as the sound waves. These vibrations are passed on to an inner eardrum by three tiny bones. From there the vibrations go to a coiled tube called the *cochlea*. This

Sound waves

Eardrum

To brain

Cochlea

tube is filled with liquid that vibrates at the same speed as the inner eardrum. The vibrating liquid has tiny hairs in it. These hairs send nerve messages to our brain. And the brain tells us that we are hearing a sound.

'Seeing' Sounds

If sound waves go into a microphone they are changed into electrical waves. These electrical waves can be seen on a screen like a television

screen. Low sounds look something like picture 1. High sounds look like picture 2. Soft sounds look like 3. And loud sounds look like 4.

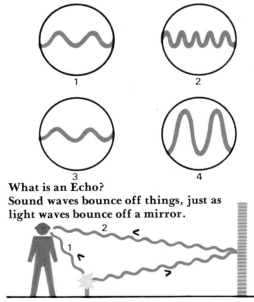

What is an Echo?

Sound waves bounce off things, just as light waves bounce off a mirror.

When the firecracker in the picture goes 'bang', some sound waves go straight to the man's ears (1). Some waves hit the wall and bounce back to the man (2). If the wall is far enough away, he hears the 'echo' from the wall after the first bang.

The Speed of Sound

Have you noticed how the musical note — the *pitch* — of a car's horn is higher when the car is coming towards you than when it is going away from you? When the car is coming towards you the sound waves from the horn are crowded together (1). More of them reach you every second. When the car is going away, the opposite happens. The sound is lower (2).

Bangs from the Skies

Some aircraft fly faster than sound waves. This causes a special noise problem. As soon as a plane like *Concorde* (below) reaches the speed of sound, the air ahead of it is disturbed. The disturbed air makes sound waves, and loud bangs are heard on the ground.

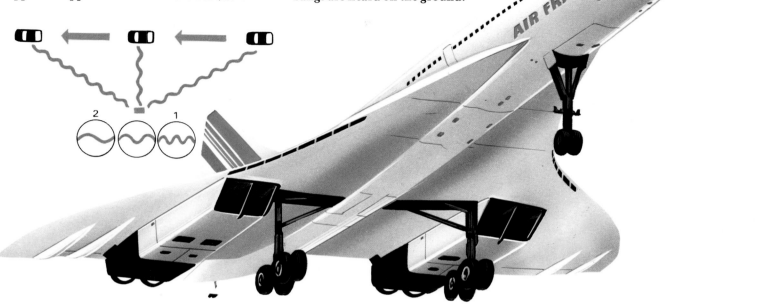

Pleasant and Unpleasant Sounds

We all know that some sounds are pleasant and others are unpleasant. Compare the pleasant sound of a violin with the harsh scraping noise of chalk on a blackboard. When the strings of a violin vibrate they make a regular pattern of

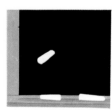

Vibrating Together

Most of the sound that comes from a violin is made by the wooden body. The wood vibrates in sympathy with the vibrations of the strings. This is called *resonance.* A glass will vibrate to a certain musical note. If the note is kept up for some time the glass may vibrate so much it shatters.

Underwater Sound

Sound waves travel through anything. They travel four times faster through water than through air. The depth of the ocean can be measured by using sound waves. A ship sends out a sound signal. The sound goes down to the bottom and bounces back up to the ship. Instruments measure the time taken for the sound to go down and come back. This gives the depth.

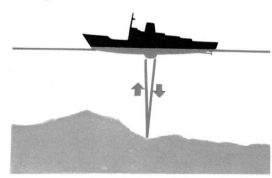

sound waves. The sound is pleasant. The scraping chalk makes no regular pattern of sound waves. The noise is unpleasant.

When a violin string is played, the whole length of the string vibrates and makes sound waves of a certain frequency. The frequency depends on how tight the string is. The tighter the string, the higher the frequency and the higher the note.

But each half of the string vibrates too. The halves vibrate faster than the whole string. They make a musical note much higher but not as loud as the whole string's sound. Other parts of the string also vibrate at different frequencies. Their different notes, which all sound at the same time, are called *overtones.* Added together, they make the pleasant sound of the violin.

Other musical instruments have different overtones. It is the overtones that help us tell the difference between instruments, even if they are all playing the same note.

The Telephone

When you speak into a telephone your voice makes a microphone vibrate. The vibrations are turned into electrical waves that whizz down the wires to the earpiece of the person you are speaking to. There a thin *diaphragm* is made to vibrate by the electrical waves. The diaphragm vibrations are the same as those of your voice.

Make a telephone with plastic cups and a piece of string. Keep the string tight and speak into one cup. Your voice waves can be heard in the other cup.

Earpiece

Diaphragm

Microphone

Atoms, Atoms, Atoms

Everything is made of atoms. Things you can see, like the wood in a table, or the paper of this page, things you cannot see, like the air, are all made of atoms. You are made of atoms, too.

If the atoms in something are packed closely together, that something is a *solid*. If the atoms in something are not so tightly packed — if they move about more — that something is a liquid like water or orange juice. And if the atoms move about a great deal, we have a gas, like air.

Simple Substances

Think how many different substances there are. You could go on counting them for weeks and never reach the end. But all these millions of different things are made up from about a hundred simple substances. These simple substances are called *elements*. Some elements are solid, like iron and gold. Others are liquids, like mercury. Some are gases, like the oxygen and hydrogen in the air.

Atoms Join Together

The atoms of elements often join together to make different substances. The salt you put on your food is made up of atoms of the elements sodium and chlorine. An atom of sodium joins with an atom of chlorine to make salt, like this:

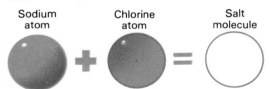

Sodium atom + Chlorine atom = Salt molecule

Two atoms of the gas hydrogen and one of the gas oxygen join together to make water. This family of hydrogen and oxygen atoms is called a *molecule* of water (below). Most things are made up of families of atoms like this.

But water is a very simple family — a simple molecule. Some molecules are very complicated. They have thousands of atoms in them. Even so, they are still far too small to see.

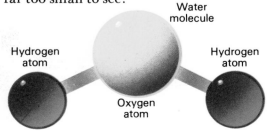

Water molecule

Hydrogen atom

Hydrogen atom

Oxygen atom

A carbon atom

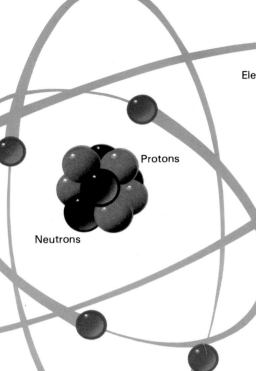

Electrons

Protons

Neutrons

In a solid, atoms pack tightly

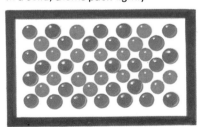

In a liquid, atoms can move about

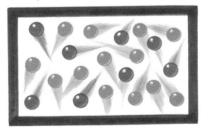

In a gas, atoms move about a lot

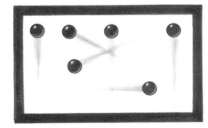

The Tiny Atom

It is very difficult to imagine how small an atom is. We cannot see them — they are far too small. Look at the period at the end of this sentence. It has in it about 250,000 *million* atoms!

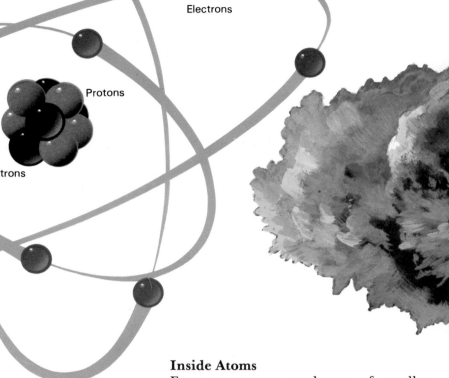

Inside Atoms

Even atoms are made up of smaller pieces. Each element is made up of its own kind of atoms. The simplest atom is

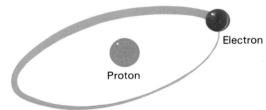

Electron

Proton

that of the gas hydrogen. (Hydrogen is a very light gas. When a balloon is filled with hydrogen, it rises into the air.)

The hydrogen atom looks something like the picture above. The center is a tiny solid body called a *proton*. Around it spins an *electron*.

Other atoms are much more complicated than the hydrogen atom. The 'lead' in pencils and burned wood are made of *carbon*. A carbon atom has 6 electrons whizzing round the center. And the center is made up of 6 protons and 6 other things called *neutrons*. It looks something like the picture at the top of this page.

The tiny electrons whizz around the center of the atom at fantastic speeds.

Using Atoms

When the center of an atom breaks up, the pieces fly apart very fast. And they make a lot of heat when they do this.

Scientists can make an atom break apart. They can make the pieces from this tiny explosion cause other atoms to break apart, and so on until there are millions of exploding atoms. This happens all of a sudden and is called a *chain reaction* (right). And if a chain reaction is not kept under control we have an atomic explosion. Atom bombs cause chain reactions in atoms out of control (below).

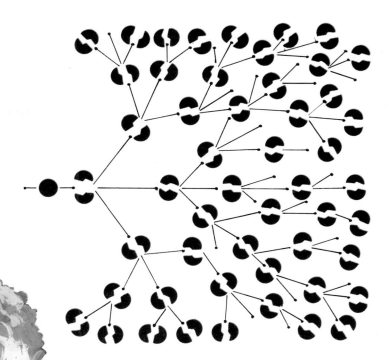

Albert Einstein
Albert Einstein was a great German scientist who died in 1955. He was the first man to say that matter can be turned into heat, or other forms of energy.

What Einstein said started the work that led up to the atomic bomb and then to atomic power stations.

Electricity from the Atom

More and more of the electricity we use comes from atomic power stations. To make useful power from the atom, scientists use a special kind of a metal called uranium. The atoms in this uranium are always breaking up and making heat. To control the amount of heat, the uranium is made into long rods. The rods are put into a *reactor core* and are separated by other rods made of carbon. With the right number of uranium rods and carbon rods, the reactor goes on making a lot of safe heat.

Water flows round inside the reactor. This water boils and the steam is made to drive turbines. The turbines make electricity. This electricity is fed into the ordinary grid system.

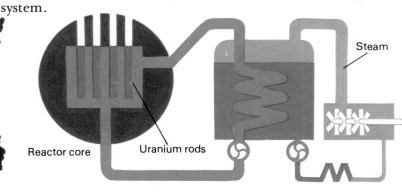

Reactor core   Uranium rods   Steam   Electric generator

Hot water

Electricity to homes and factories

In the reactor core of atomic power stations there are some rods called *control rods*. These can be moved out or in to control the chain reaction.

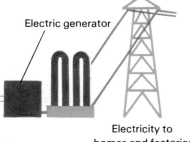

Magic Magnets

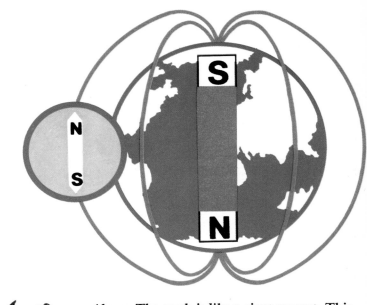

There is a story about an ancient Greek shepherd called Magnes. One day, as he tended his flock, he was surprised to find that the iron nails in his sandals were clinging to a large black stone. Magnes had discovered *magnetism*. The stone we call *magnetite*. It is a natural magnet.

The whole earth behaves as if it had a huge magnet at its center. The invisible force of this huge magnet spreads out into space all around the earth. This *magnetic field* round the earth is very important. It is because of this magnetic field that compass needles always point to the North.

Attracting and Pushing Apart

A magnet will attract metals such as iron, steel, and a few others. It will pick up pins and nails. It will not pick up pieces of wood or paper or things made of metals like copper or gold. Some magnets are quite strong; others are weak.

The ends of a magnet are called its poles. The end that points towards North is called the north pole. The other end is the magnet's south pole. We have marked the north pole with an N, the south pole with an S. The magnets in the pictures below are called bar magnets. All magnets are stronger at their ends than at their middle. They can pick up more things at their poles.

Above: The earth is like a giant magnet. This makes compass needles point North and South. Left: A piece of magnetic rock. It draws nails to it, just like a magnet.

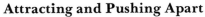

Place the north pole of one magnet near the south pole of another magnet. The magnets will stick together.

Place the south pole of one magnet against the south pole of another magnet. The magnets will push each other apart.

The magnet on the right is called a horseshoe magnet. If you hang chains of pins from it, each pin becomes a little magnet. Each one has its own poles and keeps its magnetism for a time when it is separated from the big magnet.

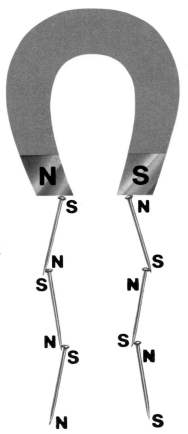

What Makes a Magnet?

To understand how a magnet works, we can imagine that it is made up of lots of tiny magnets. Before a magnet becomes magnetized, these tiny pieces are all lying in different directions. Although they are all tiny magnets, they cancel each other out. The whole bar is not a magnet. It cannot lift a pin.

If we stroke the bar with a magnet or wind a wire round it and pass an electric current through the wire, something happens. All the tiny magnets line up and point in the same direction. Their north poles point one way; their south poles point the other. We have a magnet.

Electricity Makes Magnets

If we take a piece of wire and wind it round a pencil, we have a coil of wire. When we touch each end of the coil to opposite terminals of a battery, we find that the coil becomes a magnet. As electric current from the battery runs through the coil, the coil becomes an *electromagnet*. It has a north pole and a south pole, just like a bar magnet.

If we wind the wire round a big nail instead of a pencil, the coil becomes a stronger magnet. When we pass an electric current through it, it will lift heavier things. And when we take the nail out of the coil we find that it has become a magnet too.

Electromagnets are very useful.

The crane on the left uses a powerful electromagnet to lift scrap metal. When the crane driver wants to drop the metal he just switches off the electric current.

An electromagnet is a coil of wire wound round a piece of iron. The magnet works when electricity is passed through the wire.

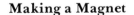

A Magnetic Field

If we lay a piece of white paper on top of a bar magnet and sprinkle iron filings on it, the filings will arrange themselves as you can see in the picture.

The iron filings show the magnetic field of the magnet. You can see that there are more filings at the poles of the magnet.

Making a Magnet

If you stroke a nail with a magnet, the nail will become a magnet too. But stroke the nail one way only. Suspend the nail and it will point to North.

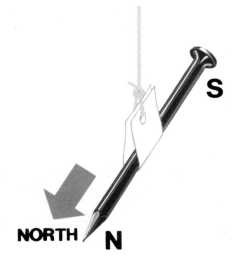

NORTH

S

N

The Shapes of Crystals

We all know what crystals look like. They have sharp corners and flat sides — like diamonds. Crystals may be of all sizes. Some are so small they can only be seen through a microscope. Others are huge. Quartz crystals as big as a man have been found.

Inside Crystals

Everything on earth is made up of very tiny atoms, or combinations of atoms called molecules. If the molecules in something are arranged in a fixed pattern, that is, repeated over and over again, that something is a crystal. The shape of the crystal you can see depends on the shape of the molecule pattern inside it.

Masses of Tiny Cubes

The salt you put on your food is called sodium chloride by chemists. It is made up of two different kinds of atoms — sodium atoms and chlorine atoms. These tiny atoms are arranged in cube patterns as you can see in the picture below. Thousands and thousands of these tiny cubes join together to make one grain of salt. And each grain of salt also wants to be a cube.

If you look at some grains of salt through a good magnifying glass you will be able to see that they are all little cubes.

Crystals often grow in large clumps like the calcite crystals above.

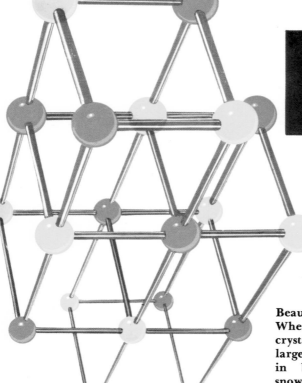

Beautiful Snow Crystals

When snow falls it is made up of tiny crystals of ice or of snowflakes that are large masses of crystals. Ice crystals form in beautiful shapes, and no two snowflakes are ever exactly the same. But they all have one thing in common. They are all six-sided.

Snow crystals are all different, but they all have six sides or points.

Next time it snows, collect some snowflakes on a dark cloth and look at them through a magnifying glass. You will be amazed at their beautiful six-sided patterns.

The Shapes of Crystals

Crystals are of many different shapes. (You can see some of the shapes on the opposite page.) But all the crystals which make up anything obey certain rules. We have seen that every tiny salt crystal tries to be a perfect cube. (Some don't manage this because they rub against their neighbors or are broken.) Crystals of copper sulfate or alum are not small cubes. They are quite different shapes. But every alum crystal tries to be the same as its neighbor.

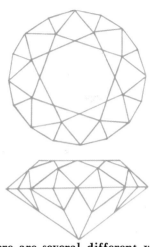

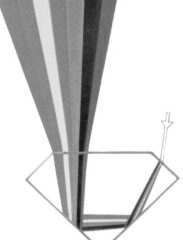

Diamonds

Diamonds are crystals. They are the hardest substance that we know of. Scientists think that these precious stones were formed millions of years ago deep inside the earth. They came to the surface in molten lava.

Many tons of rock have to be mined to find one diamond. And when they are taken from the rock, diamonds look like dull pieces of glass (above).

Cutting Diamonds

Diamonds are prized as gemstones because of their 'sparkle'. They reflect light very well and turn it into all the colors of the rainbow. But before they can do this, they have to be 'cut'. Each small face or *facet* must be just the right shape and in the right position. Diamond cutting is a very difficult job. The stones are so hard they have to be cut with tools that are tipped with other diamonds.

There are several different ways of cutting diamonds to make them sparkle. One of the most popular is shown above from the top and from the side. It is called the *brilliant* cut. In this cut there are 58 faces, each of which has to be cut and polished.

Much more common than diamonds are stones like the agate on the right. Agates are a kind of quartz, one of the commonest minerals on earth. Their beautiful colored bands are arranged in many different ways.

Below you can see some of the shapes of natural crystals.

When a ray of light goes into a diamond it hits one of the faces and is reflected to another face. Here it is reflected again and comes out, showing all the colors of the rainbow. This happens at all the diamond's faces. So the diamond sparkles.

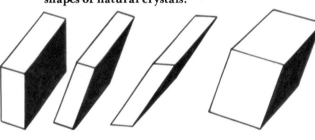

Making Crystals

Stir sugar into a little water until no more sugar will dissolve in the water. Then pour the sugary water into a saucer and leave it. As the water evaporates you will find sugar crystals forming. But these crystals will be very small and not perfect in shape.

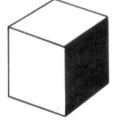

Growing a Large Crystal

To grow a perfect crystal, take some table salt or sugar or borax or alum. Alum, which can be bought from a druggist, works best. Stir your substance into hot water until no more of it will dissolve. You have made what is called a *saturated solution.* Pour the liquid into

a glass jar and leave it undisturbed for a few days. As the water evaporates, some crystals will grow on the bottom of the jar.

Pick out one of the best crystals from the bottom and hang it by a thread in a new, cooled saturated solution. Day after day you will see your crystal grow. Remove any new crystals that form in the jar.

If you use alum you will find that the crystal is shaped like two pyramids placed base to base.

Glass is Not a Crystal

Some substances that look as though they might be made of crystals are not. One of these is glass. Glass, strangely enough, is really a liquid — a liquid that is very slowly flowing all the time.

Metals all Around Us

The world would be a very funny place if there were no metals. Imagine what it would be like without iron and steel to make cars, ships, knives, rockets and machines of all kinds. And there would be no gold, silver, lead, aluminium and many other useful metals.

The First Use of Metals
People first used metals many thousands of years ago. Early man found pieces of gold in river beds and beat them into ornaments. Then he learned how to melt rocks in fires and get iron. With this metal he could make tools and weapons with quite sharp cutting edges.

Very few metals are found in the earth in the pure form we know. Gold (left below) is found by itself or embedded in other rocks, but iron has to be smelted out of rock like that shown below, right. It is called iron ore.

Beautiful Metals
All over the world, and over many centuries, men have shaped metals into beautiful objects. Gold has always been a favorite because of its shiny yellow color. It is also easy to beat into a shape like the ancient Greek mask in the picture (1). Gold does not decay or rust like some other metals. The shiny gold mask of Tutankhamen, an ancient Egyptian pharaoh, is over 3,000 years old (2).

The first metal to be found and worked was probably copper. But copper by itself was too soft, and people began mixing some tin with the copper. This made bronze, a metal that was much harder. The statue of Buddha (3) is made of bronze coated with gold.

Arms and armor have always been an important use for metals — especially iron. The beautifully decorated breastplate (4) was made in the 16th century. The swords (5) come from Japan.

METAL FACTS
Eighty-one of the 106 elements are metals.

Heat and electricity travel through metals easily — especially through silver and copper.

The metal sodium can be cut as easily as soap.

Most metals can be hammered into thin sheets — they are *malleable*. They can also be drawn out into wires — they are *ductile*.

Gold can be beaten into leaves so thin you can see through them.

Eight percent of the earth's crust is made up of aluminum.

Most metals are silvery, but a few, such as gold and copper, are colored.

Making Steel
Steel is the most important metal in the world. It is strong and can be made in different ways to do different jobs. Steel is really a mixture (an *alloy*) of iron and carbon. On the left is a huge ladle of red-hot molten steel.

Making Iron
To make iron, the ore that comes from the ground is smelted in a huge brick-lined *blast furnace*. To the ore are added coke and limestone. (A blast furnace is so called because a blast of hot air is blown through it to make the coke blaze to great heat.) The limestone helps to remove impurities from the ore. These impurities run off near the bottom of the furnace (see the picture below). The impurities are called *slag*. The molten iron runs out right at the bottom.

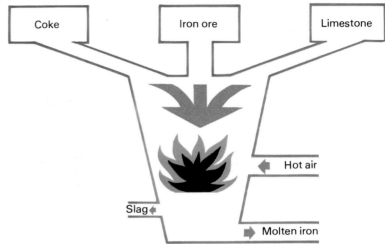

Joining Metals
Two ways of joining metals together are *riveting* and *welding*. In riveting, a metal plug with a rounded head (the rivet) goes through the holes in the parts to be joined. The other end is hammered until it also has a head which holds the pieces together. Sometimes the rivet is red hot. In welding (below right) the two pieces are heated until they melt together.

Soldering Metals Together
Soldering is another way to join metals (below). An alloy, often a mixture of lead and tin, is melted between the two pieces of metal. When the solder cools it makes a firm joint. A paste called *flux* is put in to make a better joint.

Some Common Alloys
Brass is a mixture of copper and zinc. The more zinc, the harder the brass. Bronze is a mixture of copper and tin. Statues are often made of it. Pewter is a mixture of lead and tin. It was once used for making tableware.

Unusual Metals
All metals are not hard. Mercury (below left) is a silvery liquid. It is used in thermometers and barometers. Some metals are so light they float on water.

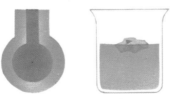

Cutting Metals
Metals can be cut by using an *oxyacetylene burner*. This kind of burner makes a very hot flame by burning acetylene gas in oxygen.

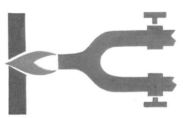

Shaping Metals
There are many ways to shape metal. A simple way is *casting* (1). Molten metal is poured into a mold. The metal hardens in the shape of the mold. *Pressing* (2) is used to shape sheets of steel. A heavy press forces the metal to the right shape. *Forging* (3) has long been used by blacksmiths. The red-hot metal is shaped on an anvil. In *rolling* (4) a white-hot piece of metal is squeezed between rollers until it is a thin sheet. In *drawing* (5) thin rods are made by pulling metal through small holes.

Electricity all Around Us

When the ancient Greeks saw lightning flashing down from the sky, they thought the god Zeus was angry. He was throwing down thunderbolts. Now we know that lightning is a flash of electricity from cloud to cloud or from the clouds to earth.

Electrons on the Move

When you walk on some carpets you get a tiny electric shock if you touch something made of metal. Your feet take some electrons from the atoms in the carpet. These extra electrons spread all over your body. You become *charged with electricity*. Then, when you touch something like a doorknob, these extra electrons jump across to the metal. There is a tiny spark and you feel a small shock. The rubbing of your feet on the carpet has made electricity.

We can think of electrons as small pieces of *negative* electricity. When electrons jump from atom to atom along a wire, we say that an electric current is flowing in the wire. It takes millions upon millions of electrons jumping along a wire to light a flashlight bulb.

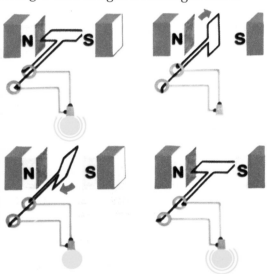

Making Electricity

Most of the electricity we use is made by *generators*. (If you have a small generator on your bicycle, it may be called a *dynamo*.)

One of the greatest discoveries of all time was made by Michael Faraday in 1831. He found that if a wire is moved through the invisible field that surrounds a magnet, an electric current flows in the wire. You can see how this works in the picture above. The electric current is greatest (the lamp lights up brightly) when the wire of the loop cuts straight across the magnetic field. (There is an invisible magnetic field between the North and South poles of the magnet.)

Michael Faraday

Michael Faraday was born in 1791. He was the first man to show that electricity is made when a wire moves through a magnetic field. So it was Faraday who gave us electric power for our homes and factories. He also did brilliant work in showing how electricity and chemistry are connected.

Making a Lot of Electricity

The very simple generator shown on the left makes very little electricity. To make enough electricity for a big town we need huge generators like those in the picture on the opposite page. Instead of one loop of wire, they have thousands. And the magnets are very strong electromagnets.

Two Kinds of Electric Current

When a piece of wire is connected to the terminals of a battery, an electric current flows through the wire. Electrons flow from the negative terminal of the battery to the positive terminal. This kind of electric current is called a *direct current,* sometimes shortened to D.C.

The current that runs through the wires in your home is not direct current. This is called *alternating current* (A.C.) because it flows first one way and then the other. It repeats this to-and-fro *cycle* 50 times every second.

Inside a Plug

Inside most plugs in your house are three wires (below). The electricity comes in from the wall socket and runs through one wire. It goes from the plug, through your lamp, and back through the other wire to the socket. The third wire, colored green and yellow, is a safety wire. It is connected to the earth.

Also in the plug is a *fuse*. Fuses are there for safety. They help prevent fires. If a wire gets too hot it will catch fire. The fuse stops this happening. It has inside it a thin piece of soft wire. If too much electricity goes through the fuse wire it melts and breaks. The electricity stops flowing.

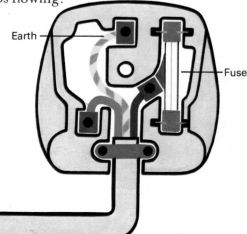

Earth

Fuse

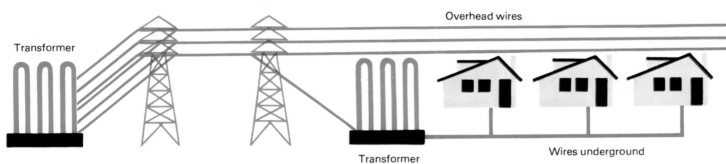

Transformer

Overhead wires

Transformer

Wires underground

Electricity Goes in a Circle

When you make electricity work for you — when it lights a lamp or makes heat to brown your toast — it has to keep moving. It flows from the big generator at the power station, through wires stretched high above the ground on pylons.

When the electricity reaches your town it goes through wires under the ground to your house. Then it runs through your lamp and back through another wire, all the way to the power station.

Electricity Don'ts

Electricity is a servant we could not do without. The picture on the right shows a few of the things it does for us. But you must treat electricity carefully, for it can be dangerous.

DON'T tamper with electrical wiring.

NEVER touch anything electrical if you are in the bathtub or your hands or feet are wet. Water allows an electric current to flow into your body more easily.

NEVER stand under a tree when there is lightning about. The lightning always chooses the easiest way to get to the ground. Through a tree is easier than going through the air.

Electricity always needs two wires. One wire brings the electricity to your lamp. The other goes back to the generator.

When electricity has to be sent over long distances, it first goes through a *transformer.* The transformer increases the *voltage* of the electricity — it gives it more push. When the electricity reaches your town another transformer brings the voltage down again so that we can use it more safely.

Batteries

The electricity that comes from batteries is made by the chemicals inside them. The dry battery you use in flashlights and transistor radios stops making electricity after a while. It cannot be recharged. But batteries like the ones in cars can be recharged again and again. Inside a car battery are lead plates in weak sulfuric acid. The picture below shows how some of the lead plates are arranged. Six groups like this would make a 12-volt battery — 2 volts from each group.

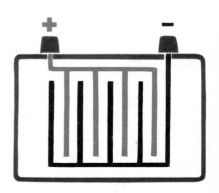

Liquid Energy

Did you know that the gas for our cars, the diesel oil for our trucks and ships, and the kerosene for our jet planes all come from the same stuff? They all come from the thick, dark, viscous oil that is found beneath the surface of the earth in some places. So do heating oil for our schools and homes, and heavy oils for 'oiling' machinery.

But these are not the only uses for oil. Chemists turn it into thousands of other useful things. They turn it into plastics, detergents, man-made fibers, explosives and many more. You can see why people spend so much time and money in finding new oil wells and in getting the valuable oil out of the ground.

What is Oil?

The oil we use today was formed millions of years ago. Plants and animals that lived in the shallow seas died and sank to the bottom. In time their remains were covered by layers of mud and sand which turned into rock. Heat and pressure turned the plant and animal remains into oil. (Some of the remains were turned into natural gas, which is often found underground beside oil. Natural gas is the gas we use in our homes.)

Finding Oil

Oil is not easy to find. But oilmen know the kind of rocks in which they are most likely to find it. They take pictures from planes, they drill holes, they set off explosions (see opposite page).

When the oilmen think they have found oil, drilling begins. If it is on land, a tall steel rig is put up. When the oil is under the sea, a huge drilling platform can be towed to the site. The platform also needs a tall rig to raise and lower the drilling pipes.

Drilling for Oil

A *bit* at the end of a long pipe is turned so that it drills into the ground. The bit is made of hard steel. It has wheels with sharp teeth. These wheels turn when the pipe is turned and bore their way into the rock. When one length of pipe is down as far as it can go, another length of pipe is joined to the end of it. Then another and another, until there may be two or three miles of pipe deep down in the earth.

Huge oil rigs like this one are used for drilling on the bottom of the North Sea. The work on these man-made islands is often difficult and sometimes dangerous. Storms can stop drilling for days on end.

The drilling bit above is the part that cuts into the rock. As the whole pipe turns, the bit's hard steel teeth turn too.

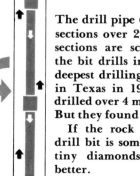

The drill pipe (left) is made up of sections over 29 feet long. These sections are screwed together as the bit drills into the earth. The deepest drilling for oil took place in Texas in 1959. There oilmen drilled over 4 miles into the earth. But they found no oil.

If the rock is very hard, the drill bit is sometimes tipped with tiny diamonds to make it cut better.

More and more of our oil is coming from under the shallow seas off the coasts of the continents.

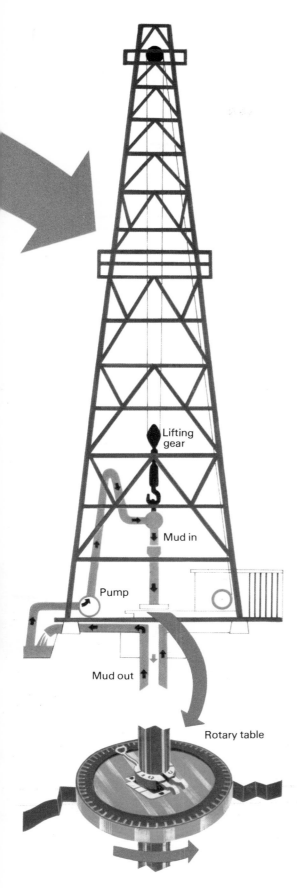

Breaking up Oil

Oil from the ground is not of much use. It has to go to an oil refinery. There it is boiled. The boiling oil goes to the bottom of a tall column (below). Different oils are collected at different levels of the column. At the bottom come heavy oils and asphalt for making roads. At the top is gas and other fuel gas.

How Oil is Found

When oilmen are searching for oil they use something called a seismograph. (Seismographs are used to tell where earthquakes are and how strong the quakes have been. They record on a piece of paper wavy lines which show any shaking inside the earth.)

Oilmen set off an explosion in the ground. The shock waves from the explosion bounce off the underground rocks. They reflect back to seismographs at different places on the surface. By looking at the wavy lines made by the seismographs, the oilmen can tell a lot about the rocks underground and whether oil may be trapped in them.

Pools of Oil

When oil was being formed millions of years ago, it dripped through *porous* rocks. (Porous rocks have tiny holes in them.) After a long time, the oil came up against solid rock and was trapped in pools. Often natural gas was formed with the oil. This was trapped too, usually just above the oil.

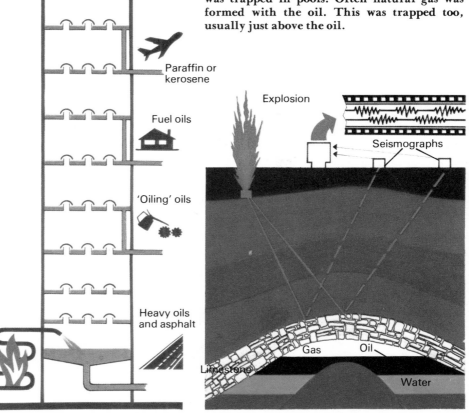

Above you can see how a drilling rig works. The lifting gear raises new sections of pipe and lowers them into place. The *rotary table* is driven round by an engine. It grips the pipe and turns it.

You can also see how soft mud is pumped down inside the pipe. The mud comes back up outside the pipe, carrying small pieces of rock with it. The mud is then cleaned of rock and pumped back down again.

To get the oil from the rigs to the refinery or to ports it is pumped through great pipes. When it has to be carried a long way, it is pumped into oil tankers. These very long ships usually have their engines, bridge and cabins in the stern. Some of them are over 1,300 feet long.

Cold Lands

The coldest places in the world are at the top and bottom of the globe. They are called the polar regions because they lie around the North and South Poles. Very few people live in these vast frozen places.

The polar bear and the walrus live in the far north. The great white bear can creep unseen across the ice, searching for seals to eat. But it will not attack the walrus. It knows to keep clear of those long tusks.

The ptarmigan is an Arctic bird. In winter its feathers are white, so that it can hardly be seen against the snow. As summer comes, the ptarmigan's feathers turn reddish brown.

Eskimos live round the Arctic circle. They kill animals and fish for food, and use animal hides to make warm clothes and tents. The men go fishing in 'kayaks'.

The Lapps also live in the Arctic. Many of them herd reindeer. The reindeer provides the Lapps with meat, milk, cheese and skins for tents, shoes and blankets.

The Arctic

The northern polar region is the Arctic. It stretches from the North Pole to the Arctic circle – an imaginary line drawn around the globe. At the very North Pole there is no land, only a huge area of frozen sea. When you fly over the North Pole, all you can see is snow and ice. In the summer the edges of this great frozen sea break up; huge icebergs drift south into the Atlantic Ocean and sailors have to keep a close look out for them.

The land in the Arctic region is frozen solid for most of the year. In the short summer the surface soil thaws and some plants can grow, even brightly colored flowers.

There are now many more people within the Arctic circle than there used to be. This is because valuable minerals have been found there – minerals such as uranium and iron. Oil has been found in the far north of Canada and oil has also been found in Alaska.

The Antarctic

The continent of Antarctica is a vast cold island at the bottom of the world. It is twice the size of Australia and is always covered by a thick layer of ice which can be as much as 2 miles thick. Scientists have found that there are great mountain ranges buried beneath this ice. The Antarctic is much colder than the Arctic. Bitter winds of 100 mph or more are quite common. There are only a very few simple plants.

The seas around Antarctica, however, teem with life. There are whales, seals, penguins, and all kinds of sea birds.

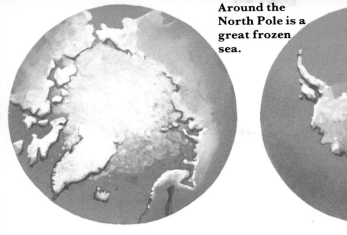

Around the North Pole is a great frozen sea.

The South Pole lies in the middle of Antarctica.

Penguins are birds that cannot fly, but they swim well. They live in the Antarctic. Here are two Emperor penguins with their chick.

The Explorers

The first man to reach the North Pole was an American called Robert Peary. With five companions and sledges pulled by dogs he reached his goal in September 1909. They had to battle for 53 days across piled-up polar ice to reach the top of the world.

The first party to reach the South Pole was led by Roald Amundsen. With 52 dogs to pull their sledges they reached the pole in December 1911.

Captain Robert Scott started for the South Pole only four days after Amundsen. He used man-hauled sledges. When Scott reached the pole after a terrible journey he found a tent set up by Amundsen. The Norwegian had beaten Scott to the pole by a month. Scott and all his men died on the way back.

Today's Polar Explorers

Brave explorers like Captain Scott died because they had very little protection against the freezing Antarctic blizzards. Today's explorers travel across the ice in huge snow-tractors. The tractors pull sledges loaded with food and scientific equipment. Some of these tractors are so big that men can eat and sleep in them.

But even with tractors, travelling in the Antarctic is dangerous. Sometimes great cracks open up in the ice. Tractor drivers must be careful.

The Midnight Sun

It is cold near the North and South Poles because the sun never rises high in the sky. In winter there are days when it does not rise at all. In summer there are days when it can be seen all day and night.

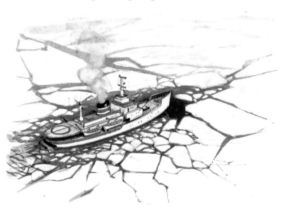

In the polar regions special ships called icebreakers are used to smash a channel of clear water through the pack ice.

There are still many dangers in Antarctic travel. This tractor is trapped in a deep crevasse which has opened up in the ice.

When Captain Scott reached the South Pole he found that the Norwegian Amundsen had got there first. Scott and his men were all frozen to death on their return journey.

Deserts

Deserts are parts of the world that have very little rain. Sometimes years pass without any rain falling. During the day it is usually very hot. At night it can become very cold. Deserts are not easy places for animals and plants to live in.

The Painted Desert
The picture below shows part of a desert in Arizona. It is called the Painted Desert because of the beautiful colors of the rock. The colors change during the day from brilliant blue to yellow and red.

Large areas of the United States are desert lands.

All Kinds of Deserts

When we think of a desert we usually think of sand, miles and miles of sand. But this is only one kind of desert. Even the great Sahara Desert in North Africa is only one-tenth sandy waste. Deserts usually have rocks and pebbles, mountains and valleys. Any large area of dry soil and rocks is a desert.

Why are deserts so dry? Usually they are dry because the winds that blow over them have lost all their moisture. Often a mountain range pushes the wind up high before it reaches the desert. As the wind rises it gets colder and forms rain. This rain falls before the wind gets to the desert. So deserts have dry winds.

By day, a desert is a boiling hot place. There are few clouds to keep out the fierce rays of the sun. At night the desert becomes cold quite suddenly. There is nothing to hold the sun's heat.

Water in the Desert

We call any fertile place in the desert an *oasis*. Some oases are small – just small clumps of palm trees round a pool of water. Others are huge areas like the whole valley of the river Nile. The picture below shows a small oasis in North Africa.

There is always water deep under the earth's surface – even beneath the driest desert. Sometimes the water comes up to the surface and makes an oasis. Caravans with heavily laden camels still travel across the desert, going from oasis to oasis.

Desert Animals

Although the desert is a cruel place to live in, there are many animals that choose to live there. The camel is the biggest of the desert animals. There are two kinds of camel. The one with one hump is called the *dromedary*, and lives in Arabia and Africa. The two-humped camel is the *Bactrian*. It lives in Asia.

The camel can live for months without drinking water. But it needs green vegetation to eat. When a camel is thirsty, it can drink over 100 quarts of water in a few minutes. The camel's big padded feet stop it sinking into the sand.

Other desert animals are wild asses, kangaroo rats with long back legs for jumping over the sand, and fennec foxes with their big ears.

There are birds in the desert too. Some fly like the owl. Others like the ostrich and the rhea cannot fly, but they can run very fast.

Animals that crawl along the ground like snakes do not often come into the open during the heat of the day. One snake often found in the American desert is the sidewinder rattlesnake. It can crawl quickly across the loose sand.

The female wolf spider lays her eggs in a silk cocoon shaped like a ball. She carries this cocoon with her wherever she goes.

Can you see all these creatures in the picture on the right?

Desert Plants

Although there is very little water around, plants still manage to live in the desert. Some desert plants have ways of storing water in their stems. Others have very long roots that go deep into the ground to catch every drop of water. Many desert plants have sharp prickles all over them. This is to stop animals from eating them to get at the water inside.

Desert People

People have learned to live in desert areas. Most desert people have dark skins. A dark skin is good protection from the sun's rays. People like the Bedouins, whom you can see in the picture on the left, wear long loose fitting robes. These help to keep them cool. The Bedouins wander from place to place looking for feeding places for their goats and sheep. Their tents are made of skin.

Very old cave paintings have been found in the Sahara. These show that the dry waterless desert was once a green and fertile land. Perhaps some day we will find ways of growing useful crops in the world's deserts.

The World's Deserts
About a fifth of all the world's land is desert. The biggest desert is the Sahara Desert in Africa. There are also big deserts in the Americas and in Asia. Most of the center of Australia is desert. You can see the world's deserts in the map above. In some deserts it rains only once in ten years.

Jungles and Forests

Forests are large areas of land which are thickly covered in trees. They form one-third of the earth's surface. There are three main kinds of forest, and trees grow everywhere except high on the tops of mountains, in the frozen lands of the Arctic and the Antarctic, and in hot, dry deserts.

Making Sure of the Future

At one time more of the earth was covered by forests than it is now. But over the ages many of them have been cleared away by man to make room for farming land. Today, forests are deliberately planted in certain places so that wood does not become too scarce. These places are called 'forestries' and they are very carefully protected. The trees are sprayed with special chemicals to kill off any harmful insects. Great care must also be taken to see that no fires start.

The wood we get from these forestries has many uses. It not only provides us with fuel and building material, but also with many other things. Some chemicals, paper, rayon and even plastics are made from wood.

Deciduous Forests

Trees which shed their leaves in winter are known as 'deciduous'. The beech, birch, oak, maple and gum are all deciduous trees. Forests of them can be found in most parts of the world where the summers are warm and the winters cool. The hard wood of deciduous trees is used for making furniture, and sports equipment such as bats and oars.

Deciduous forests provide shelter for a great many birds and animals – deer, raccoons, squirrels, badgers, wild cats, grouse and many others. Unfortunately, the deer do a lot of damage to the trees by eating the bark and trampling on young seedlings.

Coniferous Forests

Trees which do not shed their leaves in winter are called 'evergreens'. They have long, thin, needle-like leaves. These trees form their seeds in cones, so they are known as conifers. Coniferous forests are found in parts of the world where the winters are cold, such as North America and parts of Europe and Asia.

On the right you can see some of the creatures which live in coniferous forests. At the bottom of the picture there is a mink which is often hunted for its valuable fur. There are bears, elk, pumas and packs of fierce wolves. The little spiny animal on the branch above is a tree porcupine.

Jungles

The third kind of forest is called a rain-forest or jungle. Rain-forests are found in South America, Africa and parts of the east where it is very hot and there is a lot of rain. Many different kinds of trees grow in rain-forests – teak, banyan, balsa, cypress and mahogany are the most common.

Huge vines tie the trees together and brightly colored orchids and ferns grow on the branches. Where there is a clearing, perhaps beside a river, the sunlight can filter through the trees. Here the ground is covered in a dense matted undergrowth of ferns, shrubs, palms and brush.

Life in the Jungle

Most jungle animals live up among the trees. The picture on the right shows two long-limbed spider monkeys and some brightly colored macaws. They hardly ever come down on to the ground. The spotted jaguar takes to the trees when the undergrowth below is too thick for hunting. The giant anaconda snake lives near rivers. It can grow to a length of more than 22 feet.

The alligator also lives near rivers. It feeds on other animals like the little opossum which has come down from the trees for a drink.

Jungles are crawling with insects. The ants in the foreground are army ants; they travel in swarms, eating almost anything in their path.

Jungle People

Because so many of the animals live up in the trees, the jungle is not a good hunting ground for the people who live there. Many of the tribes clear small areas and grow crops such as corn, tobacco and pineapples. They trade these crops with produce from other tribes.

The people you see below are called pygmies. They live in the jungles of Africa. They only grow to about 5 feet tall. While the men hunt for food with their poisonous darts and bows and arrows, the women gather nuts, berries and honey. When the food supply runs low, pygmies move camp to another part of the jungle. But today, they are gradually losing their territory as more and more jungle is being cleared away to make room for roads and cities.

Plantations

Over the centuries, parts of the jungle have been cleared away by settlers. In these clearings, crops such as rubber, tobacco, rice, cocoa and sugar are grown. These places are called 'plantations'.

The picture above is of a rubber plantation. The rubber, in a liquid form called 'latex', is being collected from the rubber trees. The latex is taken to a collecting station where it will be turned into rubber.

39

Mountains

Almost a fifth of all the world's land is covered by mountains. And most of the high mountains are in groups such as the Himalayas in Asia. Other important mountain ranges are the Rockies and Andes in the Americas and the Alps in Europe.

Mountain Making

Mountains are made by the very slow movements of the earth's crusty surface. These movements can form different types of mountains. There are 'folded' mountains, like the Alps in Europe (picture right). They look like great waves of rock.

'Block' mountains occur where the earth has moved and broken up into huge blocks of rock. The Sierra Nevada are block mountains.

The famous Black Hills of Dakota are called 'dome' mountains. They look like enormous 'blisters'.

When a mountain is first formed, and at its highest, it is called a 'young' mountain. Mount Everest is a young mountain. It is 29,000 feet high and is the tallest in the world. As the years go by, mountains become worn down by the wind and rain to a medium height of around 6,500 feet. They are then called 'mature' mountains. After millions of years mountains become so worn down that they are little more than rolling hills.

Underwater Mountains

Mountains are not only found on the land, but also under the sea. The ocean bed is covered with mountains, plains and deep valleys. Many islands in the Pacific are really the tips of underwater volcanoes which stick out above the surface of the sea. Huge upheavals have raised them from the sea bed millions of years ago. The highest mountain on earth from its bottom to its top is not really Everest. It is Mauna Kea, on the island of Hawaii in the Pacific. But only about 13,000 feet is above sea-level.

Volcanoes

Some mountains have a hole in their center. This hole goes deep down into the earth. At the bottom of the hole is red hot liquid rock called *lava*. These mountains are called volcanoes.

When the lava shoots out of the hole at the top of the volcano we say it is *erupting*. With the lava come pieces of rock and ash. As the lava flows down the side of the mountain in a red hot stream it cools and hardens. This is how the mountain is built up over millions of years.

Some volcanoes erupt often, some very seldom and some never erupt at all. These last ones are extinct.

Traveling on a Mountain

In the past, mountain ranges have acted as barriers between countries because they were difficult to cross. Modern building methods and inventions have solved this problem. The longest rail tunnel in the world is almost 12 miles long. It is called the Simplon tunnel and it runs through the Alps between Switzerland and Italy.

Also in the Alps there is a vast network of electric railways. The trains sometimes speed along so fast that passengers say they cannot see the beautiful mountain scenery.

Steep mountain slopes make life for the motorist very difficult. Roads zig-zag their way up in a series of steep sided hair-pin bends. For shorter and easier journeys, many people travel in cable cars. These are small carriages which run along strong wires hung between towers.

Avalanches

The first snow fall of winter brings danger to every living thing on a mountain. The snow piles up on the steep slopes and one slight disturbance can cause it to crash down the mountainside at a frightening speed. This great fall of snow is called an *avalanche*. The destruction it causes can be terrible. On some mountains, special fences have been put up to keep the snow in place. You can see an avalanche in the picture.

Skiing and Climbing

The first skis were probably made thousands of years ago from large animal bones. There is a pair of skis on show in a Swedish museum which are thought to be five thousand years old. Skis have often been used by troops in times of war. But it was not until the early 1800s that skiing first became a sport. Today, millions of holiday makers go each year to ski resorts all over the world.

In ancient times mountains were feared by men and few peaks were climbed before the last century. Mountain climbing has now become a very popular sport. Most of the world's great peaks have been explored and climbed.

Before and After the Dinosaurs

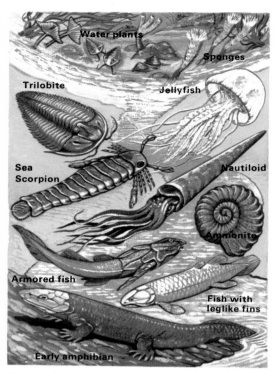

Some of the creatures that lived in the sea before the first land animals appeared.

Before people lived on the earth, it was the home of many fantastic creatures. Dinosaurs ruled our planet for more than 100 million years – fifty times longer than we have been here.

Life in the Sea

About 600 million years ago the first living things appeared in the sea. Tiny plants and soft creatures, like little blobs of jelly, were wafted about by the waves. Soon the sea was full of animals. Trilobites crawled over the sea bed feeding on smaller creatures. Huge sea scorpions seized other animals in their long, sharp claws and giant octopus-like creatures strangled passing victims with tentacles that poked out from their hard shells. The first fishes had thick armor that protected them from the sea scorpions.

From Fins to Feet

The first living things on land were plants that grew along the water's edge. Fishes swam into the shallows to eat the insects that crawled over the plants. Some of the fishes could breathe out of water and they had strong fins which they could use as legs. On land there were no enemies to eat them, so they stayed there and slowly they changed into amphibians – the first land animals. But they could not go far from the water because they needed water to lay their eggs in.

Stone Bones
We know about the animals that lived before people were there to see them from fossils. Fossils are the remains of animals that have been preserved in the rocks. When they died, the soft parts of their bodies decayed but the bones sank into the mud and were buried. Lying hidden in the ground they slowly turned to stone. Millions of years later people found the stone bones, chipped them from the rocks, and put them all back together exactly as they would have been when the animal was alive. By looking at animals that are alive today, we can even tell what the outside of their bodies must have looked like.

Brontosaurus, a giant plant-eater.

Pteranodon was a flying reptile that caught fish in its great beak.

Tyrannosaurus, the fiercest of all dinosaurs.

The Dreaded Dinosaurs

The first animals that could lay eggs on land were the reptiles. The greatest of all the reptiles were the dinosaurs. The name dinosaur means 'terrible lizard', but though many dinosaurs were enormous not many were terrible. Most of them were peaceful plant-eaters. Brontosaurus weighed 30 tons and was more than 65 feet long, but it could only plod slowly and had to spend nearly all its time eating to fill its huge stomach.

The fiercest of the dinosaurs was a meat-eater called Tyrannosaurus. It stood 19 feet high and ran on its huge back legs. It used the big claws on its small front legs for gripping its prey while it sank its dagger-like teeth into the flesh.

The Death of the Dinosaurs

Dinosaurs ruled the world for more than 100 million years. Then suddenly they died out. Nobody knows why, but many scientists think that the world became too cold for them. The animals that took their place were mammals. They had hair to keep them warm and were the most intelligent of all animals.

Two armored plant-eating dinosaurs. Stegosaurus defended itself by swinging its spiked tail like a club. Triceratops charged its enemies with its horns.

Archaeopteryx was the first known bird. It evolved from the reptiles and was like a reptile in many ways. It had teeth in its beak, scales on its head and claws on its wings. And even though it had feathers, it could not fly very well.

The hairy mammoth was a mammal that lived during the Ice Age after the dinosaurs had died out.

A.T.Riley

The Undersea World

Men have explored nearly all the land surface of the earth. Only now are they beginning to find out about the vast world below the surface of the seas.

Men are going deeper and deeper into the strange, dark depths. Skin divers (1) can go down more than 200 feet. Divers wearing helmets and with air pipes to the surface (2) can reach below 500 feet. Ordinary submarines can cruise at 2,000 feet. A very special submarine called a bathyscaphe (3) has been down about 36,000 feet (almost 7 miles). But going down very deep is not easy. Men have to be well protected against the enormous crushing pressure of the water. And, of course, they have to take their own air and light with them. It is completely black in the depths.

Deep Sea Fish

The fish of the deep ocean are very strange creatures. Most of them have huge mouths and sharp teeth with which they attack anything they meet. Fish like the deep-sea angler (4) lure other fish into their jaws with a small light on the end of a rod on top of their head. Others have patterns of lights along their sides (5 and 6). These lights help the fish to recognize each other in the dark. Some of the deep-sea fish are very long and thin. The snipe eel (7) is one of these. But none of the deep-sea creatures is very large. They are mostly small animals like shrimps (8).

The Middle Waters

To find really big creatures we have to move up to the middle waters of the sea. There is the colorful roosterfish (9), which can be 16 feet long, and the fierce Moray eel (10). But the biggest by far are the whales. We know that sperm whales (11) battle in the deep waters with giant squids (12). These huge creatures can have tentacles over 22 feet long and as thick as a man's thigh.

The Top Level

In shallow waters we find the sharks (13), the sawfish (14), and the swordfish (15). The tuna (16) is caught and used as food. But the main food fish are those like the herring and the cod which are caught in large numbers by trawlers (17). Other fish in the picture are the huge, but harmless, manta ray (18), the fun-loving dolphin (19) and the curious sunfish (20). Leaping from the surface are the flying fish (21) found in tropical waters. They have been seen to stay in the air for as long as 40 seconds.

The World of Plants

Plants make up a very large and important part of nature. There are more than 360,000 kinds of plants. Some plants are so small that they can only be seen through a microscope. Others are over 300 feet tall and may live for thousands of years. Without plants there would be no life on Earth. They use sunlight to make food and energy from the soil. Animals can then get their food by eating plants. Some of these animals are, in turn, eaten by other animals.

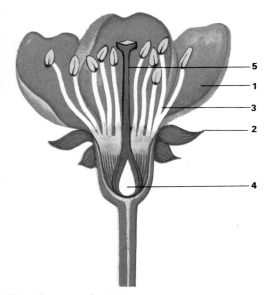

The Parts of a Flower

1. The *petals* are often brightly colored to attract insects.

2. The *sepals* are like small leaves under the petals. When the flower was a bud, the sepals were on the outside to protect it.

3. The male parts (*stamens*) produce pollen in small containers (*anthers*) on the ends of long stalks.

4. The female part has a chamber (*ovary*) that contains the egg. The seed eventually grows here.

5. The stalk (*stigma*) on the top of the ovary receives pollen from the stamens of another flower.

Autumn berries are a useful supply of food for birds. But when the birds take the berries, they are also helping the plant. They help to spread the seeds by carrying them far away.

How Plants Produce Seeds

Flowers are needed so that plants can produce seeds. These eventually grow into new plants. In this way, plants make sure that their kind continues to exist.

The first stage in making a seed is called *pollination*. Pollen is taken from the anthers of one flower to the stigma of another. Some plants are pollinated by the wind. The wind blows pollen from one flower to another.

Most plants, however, are pollinated by insects. On a sunny day you can see many insects, especially bees and butterflies, flitting from one flower to the next. They are attracted by the bright color of the petals and by the scent of nectar. When an insect enters the flower to drink the nectar, it brushes against the anthers and picks up pollen on its body. The insect then flies to another flower, where it leaves some of the pollen stuck to the top of the stigma.

One pollen grain on the stigma now produces a thin tube. This grows down through the stigma until it reaches the ovary. Here, the male cell of the pollen joins up with the female egg cell. This is called fertilization. The ovary, with the fertilized egg inside it, then grows into a seed.

All plants need water, but some plants actually grow in water. Water lilies, bulrushes and duckweed are all water plants that grow in ponds or slow-moving streams.

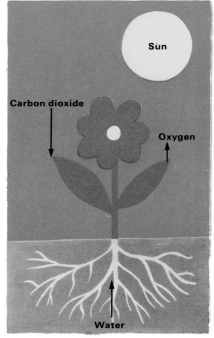

Food and Water

A plant makes its food using sunlight and carbon dioxide, which is one of the gases in the air. The leaves of a plant are green because they contain a material called chlorophyll. Carbon dioxide enters the leaves. The sunlight acts with the chlorophyll to turn carbon dioxide and water into plant food. At the same time oxygen comes out of the leaves. This is useful to animals because it is the gas they breathe.

A plant gets its water from the soil. It enters the roots and passes up the stem. Any water that the plant does not need passes out of the leaves.

Mushrooms and toadstools are unusual plants. They are not green because they do not contain any chlorophyll. Unlike green plants, therefore, they cannot make their own food. They have to get their food from rotted material in the ground.

Spreading the Seeds

Plants often make large numbers of seeds. When they are ready, they must be spread over as wide an area as possible. This is so that each seed will have the best possible chance of growing into a new plant.

Many plants have extremely clever ways of making sure that their seeds travel as far as possible. Poppy seeds are shaken, a few at a time, from a capsule that is rather like a pepper pot. The seeds are small and light and can be carried quite far by the wind. Dandelion seeds have tiny parachutes that allow the wind to carry them even farther. Sycamore seeds have wings so that, instead of falling straight to the ground, they float away from the tree as they fall.

Many seeds are spread by animals. Burrs are fruits that have tiny hooks. When an animal brushes against the plant, the burrs, with the seeds inside them, catch onto the animal's fur. They may then be carried a long way before dropping off. Other fruits are attractive – to animals as well as humans. Many berries are picked from plants by birds. The seeds inside the berries may be carried for many miles before being dropped.

Animals and plants are useful to each other. Bees and butterflies find nectar in flowers. At the same time, they pollinate the flowers, which can then make seeds. Rabbits eat plants and are usually thought of as pests. But, by carrying seeds in their fur, they help to spread plants across the countryside.

Insects and Spiders

There are more kinds of insects than all other animals added together. Butterflies, moths, ants, beetles and bees are just a few. Nobody knows for certain how many kinds there are because every day new kinds are discovered. Some are so small that you can hardly see them, while the largest, the goliath beetle, is the size of a man's fist. Spiders are not insects. They have eight legs instead of six and their bodies have two parts instead of three. The largest spiders are the hairy bird-eating spiders that live in South America.

The scorpion is a relative of the spider. It runs very fast and catches its prey with its strong claws. Then it poisons the victim with the sting in the end of its tail.

A hoverfly trapped in the web of a garden spider.

If you go out into the countryside and look carefully, you will see many of the insects in this picture. If you see a bumblebee like this one carrying loads of red pollen on its legs, you will know that it has been feeding at its favorite flower, the red clover.

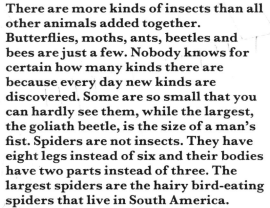

A damsel fly

A grasshopper

A plant-eating bug.

Two ants 'talking' to each other.

A Closer Look at Insects

Insects do not have skeletons inside their bodies like ours. They have a hard outer case to protect them. The three parts of their bodies are jointed so that they can move easily and their six legs also have joints. Most insects also have two pairs of wings. Some are big and beautiful like a butterfly's. Others are stiff and strong like a beetle's. Insects normally have two feelers on their heads. They use them mostly to smell and find their way about. Ants also use them to 'talk' to each other by rubbing them together.

If you look closely at an insect's eyes, you will see that they are very different from our own. Their eyes are made up of hundreds of tiny cone-shaped 'lenses'. Each one looks in a slightly different direction and works like a separate eye. The result is that objects look blurred to insects even though they can sense movement very well.

The crab spider has a cunning way of catching its food. It waits in a flower and seizes visiting insects. The insects have no chance of seeing it there because its body is exactly the same color as the petals of the flower.

A monarch butterfly and its caterpillar.

The ladybirds' bright color warns other animals that they are poisonous to eat.

Male stag beetles fight together for the females with their big antlers.

Animal Life Stories

Butterfly

Bee · Salmon · Dragonfly

Daddy longlegs · Frog

Different kinds of animals have very different life stories. The young of a mammal grows inside the mother's body until it reaches a certain size. When it is born, it looks like an adult, except that it is smaller and more helpless. But a caterpillar, which is the young of a butterfly, looks nothing like the adult. Like many insects it must go through a great change (called metamorphosis) before it becomes an adult butterfly. Not all insects, however, need to go through this great change during their life story. The young of the silverfish (shown above) looks like its parent when it emerges from the egg. It then just grows until it reaches the adult size.

The pictures above show the adults of six animals, and their young are below. Read the life stories on this page and try to guess which young belong to which adults. The young dragonfly is on the left.

Honey bees make a nest that consists of thousands of compartments (1). The queen bee lays eggs in empty compartments (2). An egg hatches out into a grub. This lives inside its compartment, where it is fed by adult bees (3). After a while, it changes into a pupa (4). Eventually, the insect emerges from the pupa as a fully grown adult (5).

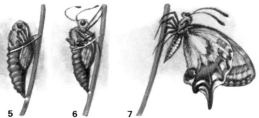

A butterfly lays its eggs on the underneath of leaves (1). When the egg hatches, a caterpillar emerges. It feeds first on the leaf where the egg was laid, and then moves on to other leaves (2).

After a few weeks it finds a suitable place to rest, forms a hard case over itself (3), and becomes a chrysalis or pupa (4). Inside the chrysalis a great change takes place. Eventually the adult

butterfly breaks open the top of the case, and starts to emerge (5, 6). When it is completely out of the case it rests for a while until its wings unfold.

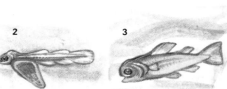

A salmon lays its eggs in the shallow water of streams far inland (1). Very young salmon are called fry (2), which live among the stones of the stream.

When they have grown larger, they are called parr (3). The parr swim downstream to the sea, where they become adult salmon (4). When it is

time for the breeding season to begin again, the adult salmon swim back up the rivers, sometimes leaping up waterfalls (5).

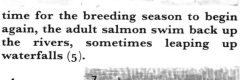

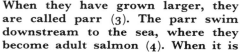

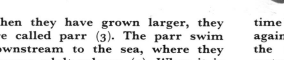

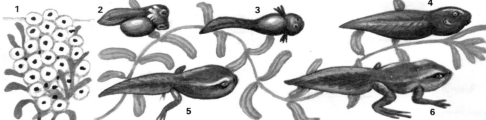

A frog lays its eggs on weeds in ponds and streams (1). After a while a tadpole hatches out of the egg (2). For a few weeks the tadpole has fringe-like organs (called gills) on the outside of

its body. These are used for taking in oxygen from the water (3). As the tadpole grows, it loses its outside gills (4). After about three months, the tadpole goes through a series of

remarkable changes. The most obvious change is that legs develop (5, 6). Gradually the tail disappears. The adult frog is now able to leave the water and climb on to the land (7).

Reptiles

Most reptiles lay eggs with hard shells. They do not look after their young. In fact the parents of most reptiles are not usually around when the eggs hatch. Turtles lay their eggs on sandy beaches. They bury them under the sand and then leave them. Alligators, on the other hand, make a rough kind of nest. The mother lays her eggs and then waits until the young are ready to hatch. She then helps them to emerge by breaking the shells.

Birds

Like the reptiles, birds also lay eggs. Many birds build nests in which to lay their eggs. But the great difference between birds and reptiles is that birds look after both the eggs and the young.

An egg is laid while the young bird is growing inside. It gets its food from the yolk of the egg. The shell of the egg allows air to pass through into a space at one end. Blood vessels carry oxygen from this space to the growing bird.

Eggs are kept warm by the female bird, who sits on them until they hatch. Sometimes the male bird also takes a turn at sitting on the nest. When the eggs hatch, the young birds are completely helpless. The parents spend most of their time searching for food, to feed their young. When the young birds are old enough, they leave the nest and fly away.

Mammals

All mammals take great care of their young. The mother feeds the young with her milk and continues to look after them until they are able to fend for themselves.

The most primitive mammals are called *Monotremes*. There are only two kinds – the duck-billed platypus and the spiny anteater. They are the only mammals that lay eggs.

Marsupials are more advanced mammals. They include kangaroos, koala bears, and possums. The young grow inside the mother's body. But they are born in a very weak state. After birth, they crawl through the mother's fur until they reach the pouch, where they remain for some time.

The true mammals vary a great deal in shape, size, and way of life. They include humans, cats, dogs, rabbits, mice and whales. But they all have one main thing in common. The young are kept inside the mother's body until they have grown to a considerable size.

Animal Friends and Enemies

In the savage world of nature, where the hunter often becomes the hunted, animals wage a constant battle to eat but not be eaten themselves.

For plant-eaters, finding food is not normally difficult. But not becoming food themselves often is. Most animals flee from their enemies. Only a few stand their ground and fight, and they normally have protective horns or armor.

For meat-eaters, finding food is more difficult simply because their victims always do their best to escape. To catch food they need speed and skill. A lion must quietly stalk its victim without letting the hunted animal catch its scent. And it must close in swiftly for the kill.

Everyone knows how difficult it is to catch a fly. Imagine how much more difficult it must be for a fish. Yet the archer fish has no trouble. It brings down flies by shooting a jet of water droplets at them as they fly over the surface or crawl on the waterweeds.

Low Cunning

For both hunter and hunted, cunning is often of more use than speed. The garden spider makes a web of sticky silk and sits in a nearby hideaway to wait for its victims to walk or fly into the trap. The praying mantis keeps per-fectly still as it waits in leaves as green as its body. Neither its victims nor its enemies know that it is there.

Many insects are protected by their color or by their shape. There are moths that look like bark or dead leaves, caterpillars like pine needles, mantises like flowers, leaf insects like leaves, tree hoppers like thorns and stick insects like thin twigs. They look so like the plants they live on that their enemies pass them by without a second glance.

Safety in Numbers

Often living and feeding together is the safest way for animals to live. A meat-eater would rather attack an animal on its own than take on a whole herd. And in a herd, too, there are more animals to watch and warn the others when danger threatens. Some animals hunt together. In the Arctic, packs of wolves search for weak or wounded musk oxen to attack. But the musk oxen have a good defense. They herd the young ones together and form a tight circle around them. With their horns lowered they face the howling wolves who soon give up and go away.

As soon as it feels its prey touch the web, the garden spider rushes out of hiding, wraps the victim in silk and digs its poisonous fangs into the animal's helpless body.

The archer fish stuns its prey with a jet of water, shot with an aim as swift and sure as an archer's.

A herd of zebra gallop away from a hunting lioness. Without a good start, they could not possibly outrun her powerful strides. Their safety hangs only on the chance that she will tire first.

Protecting their young, a herd of musk oxen stand their ground against a pack of hungry wolves.

In the picture on the right there are twelve insects that look like parts of plants. Can you find them all?

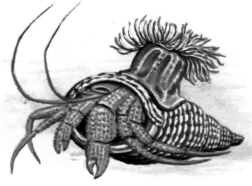

A sea anemone hitches a lift with a hermit crab.

A Favor for a Friend

Animals of the same kind often live together and help each other. But it is unusual for two different kinds of animals to do so. Most animals keep well away from crocodiles, but the Egyptian plover knows that it can safely walk all over the dangerous beasts. This is because it feeds on parasites that live on the crocodile's skin. Glad to be rid of the pests, the crocodile even lets the birds peck about inside its great gaping jaws.

The hermit crab has no shell of its own so it lives inside the shell of a dead sea snail. Any sea anemone lucky enough to be attached to the shell is carried around by the crab, and can find more food. The crab's enemies see only the sea anemone and keep clear of the stinging tentacles.

Egyptian plovers 'clean' the teeth of a Nile crocodile.

Animal Homes

Some animals make their homes where they find them, resting briefly under a pile of stones or a heap of leaves. But others work with care and skill to construct more lasting homes.

Nest Builders

Most animals only build a home when it is time to bring up their young. Many birds weave twigs, grass and feathers together to make cup-shaped nests. Others are even cleverer. The tailor bird sews two leaves together and fills them with fluffy plant material to make a warm, soft cradle for its eggs.

The great crested grebe builds a floating nest of reeds.

Living Together

Honeybees live and work together. They build their nest with wax. The nest is a honeycomb of cells. In some cells eggs are laid and grubs reared. In others nectar and pollen are stored so there is always a good supply of food.

The Master Builders

Beavers are always busy building. First they cut down trees with their strong front teeth. They eat the bark and use the wood to make a dam across a stream. A pond of calm water collects behind the dam. In the middle of the pond the beavers build their 'lodge'. The lodge is a platform of twigs and mud that rises out of the water and is covered with a roof of branches. The entrances to the lodge are underwater. Once inside, the beavers are warm and dry and their enemies cannot cross the water to reach them.

Towns Beneath the Prairies

Prairie dogs are small mammals that live on the plains of North America. They build their homes in burrows under the ground.

The 'rooms' of the burrow are lined with straw and connected by tunnels. Each new family adds new burrows to the old ones so that often great underground towns grow up, stretching over many acres.

The house martin makes a mud nest.

The tailor bird sews its nest with plant fibers.

A weaver bird with its nest of woven grasses.

A song thrush on its basket-shaped nest.

A tiny humming bird with a nest the size of a walnut.

The ringed plover scrapes a hole in the ground to lay its eggs in.

The oven bird's nest is like an old-fashioned oven.

The woodpecker makes its nest by drilling into the trunk of a tree with its beak. The hole may be 12 inches deep.

Squirrels nest in dreys high in the trees. The drey is an untidy collection of twigs and moss. The squirrel pushes its way inside and then covers up the entrance hole.

When they are outside feeding, the prairie dogs have to post guards by the entrances to the tunnels to stop snakes getting in. When their enemy the prairie falcon flies over, they all rush underground to escape.

Prairie falcon

Badgers dig deep burrows called sets under the ground. There are several entrances and many tunnels. The 'rooms' are lined with straw. Each spring the tidy badgers throw out the old straw and replace it with new.

A Diving Bell for Baby Spiders

Land animals cannot breathe under water. But even so the water spider builds its home in a pond. First it jumps on the water and catches a bubble of air. Then it dives down and makes a silk web among the waterweeds. It fills the web with bubbles of air until it looks like a dome. Then the female spider lays her eggs in it. The young spiders have plenty of air to breathe when they hatch.

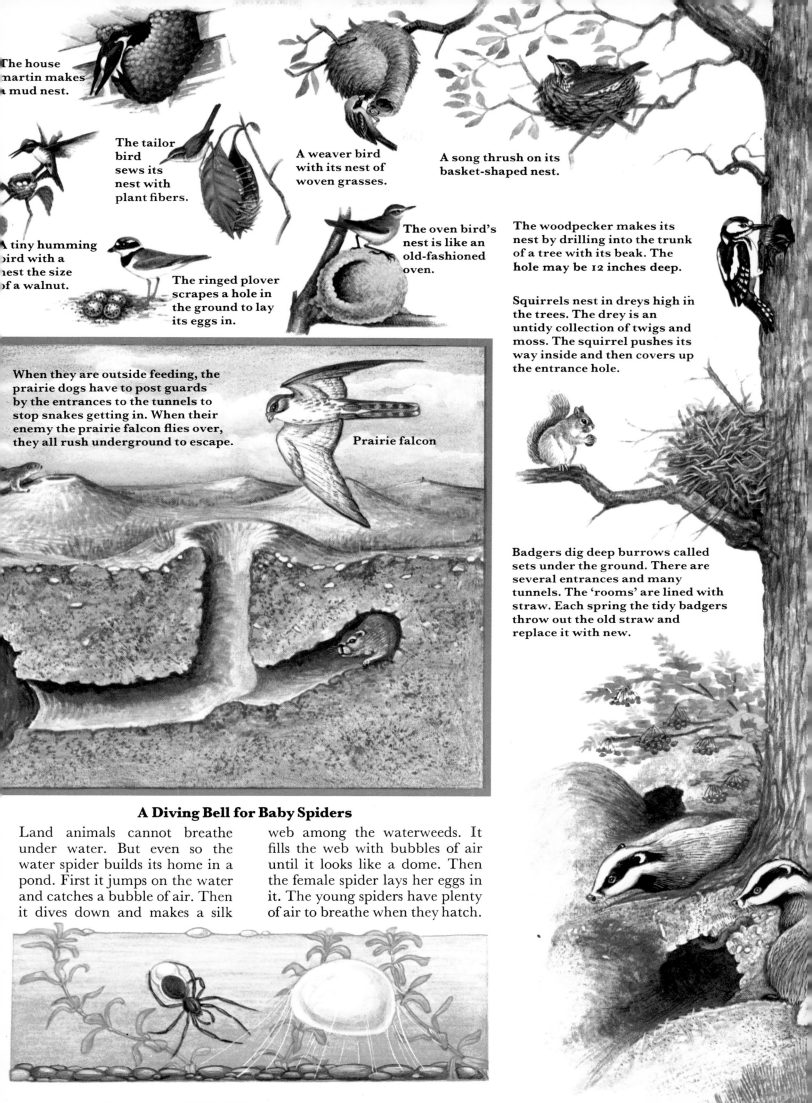

The First Men

The people in this picture look much more like apes than like us. But they are in fact our ancestors. They lived about 2 million years ago.

Scientists have traced our family tree back to apelike creatures that lived in the forests and moved about on all fours. Very, very slowly our ancestors became more manlike. They started to move on two feet. This meant that their hands were free for making and carrying things. Their brains got bigger and bigger which made them cleverer than other animals. And they learned how to talk.

Man's Ancestors
All that is left of these very early ancestors is some bones. But from them we can build up a picture of them and of how they lived. The people in the picture lived in Africa. They were just over 3 feet tall. They moved about on two feet, but probably shuffled along rather clumsily.

These early people had no homes. They moved about the country looking for food. They ate seeds, nuts, berries, and roots. Some of them killed and ate animals. But they had to eat them raw since they had no fire. To cut them up they used tools made from pebbles. They chipped away one side of the pebble to make a sharp edge.

Modern Man Appears
The first men who looked really modern had a very hard life. Many places were much colder than now. Some people sheltered in caves. Others made tents of animal skins propped up on branches or huge bones. And some people lived in pits in the ground which they roofed over with branches and earth.

People still had no settled homes. They moved round after the herds of animals – reindeer, bison, and mammoth. Often they would camp in the same place year after year when there was plenty of food there. They hunted animals with flint-tipped spears. They cut up the meat easily with sharp stone cutters. Then they scraped the skins clean. They sewed them together with bone needles to make warm clothes. They probably wore loose tunics and trousers like those of Eskimos. Sometimes they decorated their clothes with rows and rows of little bone beads. They made bone bracelets, and necklaces of bones and teeth.

The man on the right looks much more like us. He lived about a million years ago. He stood really upright and knew how to use fire for scaring away animals, cooking food, and keeping himself warm. This meant that he could live in cool places.

How Early Man Cooked
Meat was roasted over the fire. Men could not make stews because they did not know how to make pots. They heated water by putting it in a skin bag and dropping in hot pebbles. As well as meat, they ate seeds and nuts, berries and roots just like the earlier men in Africa. They fished in the rivers.

These people are man's ancestors. They lived in Africa some two million years ago. Although they look more like apes they are behaving in a manlike way making and using tools, and walking upright.

Some tools fashioned by early men from the stones around them. The earliest ones were crudely chipped, but later ones were shaped by skillfully tapping away thin flakes of the stone. All sorts of shapes were produced from large all-purpose hand-axes to delicate arrowheads.

Early Artists

Men did not know how to make pots of clay. But they used it to make models of animals – bears and lions – and of people. They also carved figures of bone. Sometimes they carved the figures of animals they hunted on rocks near the mouths of caves. Deep inside the caves they painted wonderful pictures of the animals. They drew outlines in black. Then they colored them in with red, yellow, and brown earths. Sometimes they dipped their hands in the earth and pressed them against the walls to leave handprints. Nobody knows just why they painted these pictures. Perhaps they were a sort of hunting magic.

This way of life came to an end when the weather became warmer. The herds of animals moved away to new cool areas. But men did not follow them. Instead, they learned how to raise animals in fields. They learned how to sow seeds and grow crops just where they wanted them. Now they could settle down and build proper homes. They learned how to make pots by coiling a 'sausage' of clay round and round and then smoothing it over. And they learned how to weave cloth. They had changed from wandering hunters to village farmers.

This painting of a spotted horse comes from deep inside a cave in France. The outline has been drawn in black against a background of pale rock. Above the horse is a hand print. The artist probably put his hand against the wall and then blew powder round it.

Your Body

Your body is made of millions of tiny cells. It has a covering of skin, and a framework of bones. Inside there are different parts which allow us to move, breathe, speak, eat, and sleep. Our ears, eyes and other senses tell the brain what is going on outside our bodies. The brain controls everything that we do. In fact all the parts of our bodies work together to make the most perfect machine in the world.

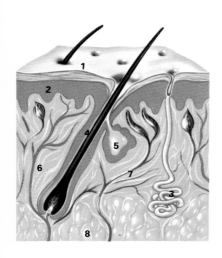

Above is a cut-away view of the skin, showing: 1. Surface 2. Epidermis 3. Sweat gland 4. Hair 5. Sebaceous gland 6. Blood 7. Nerve 8. Fat. The nerve endings in the skin help us to feel cold, hot and pain.

* The lungs can hold from 3 to 5 quarts of air. About half a quart is taken in at each breath.
* Blood takes about a minute to go from the heart, around the body, and back to the heart again.
* The skin covering the body measures almost $2\frac{1}{2}$ square yards.
* We have between 90,000 and 140,000 hairs on our heads.
* An average adult, in one day, drinks about $1\frac{1}{2}$ quarts of liquid and eats about $3\frac{1}{2}$ lb of food. He breathes about 23,000 times.
* An adult's brain weighs about $3\frac{1}{2}$ lb.
* If all the blood vessels in a human body were laid end to end they would stretch for nearly 99,000 feet.

The Skin
The skin is a waterproof covering that protects the body. It keeps us warm when it is cold and cool when it is hot. It helps us to get rid of waste water by sweating. And it acts as a strong barrier against germs.

The skin is only 4 hundredths of an inch thick. The part you can see is made of dead cells that flake off all the time. They are too small for us to see. Underneath there are two layers and some fat.

The layer of skin under the surface has a pattern of ridges and dents. You can see the pattern on your finger tips. The pattern you are born with never changes. And no one else in the world has finger-prints exactly like yours.

Muscles
The joints can only move because they have muscles attached to them, which pull them into the right position. Muscles work in pairs. To raise the lower part of your arm, one muscle contracts (gets smaller) and pulls the bone up. The other muscle is relaxed. To lower your arm the first muscle relaxes and the other one contracts (above).

The Skeleton
If you did not have a skeleton you would be just a flabby blob, unable to stand up. The skeleton is a framework of more than 200 bones, linked by joints. The joints allow us to move. Some work like hinges. The bones at a joint are held together by stretchy ligaments.

Breathing
When you run fast, you sometimes get out of breath. This is because your muscles have used up their oxygen. Oxygen is a gas and is part of the air we breathe in. Without it our bodies cannot work.

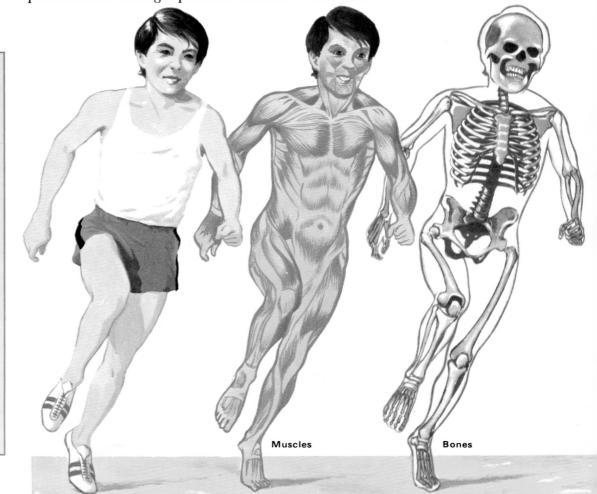

Muscles   Bones

Oxygen is taken into our lungs when we breathe and is carried to all parts of the body by the blood. We would die very quickly without it.

The lungs suck air into the body and blow it out like a pair of bellows. The blood absorbs the oxygen from the lungs and takes it to other parts of the body.

When we breathe out, air passes through a part of the windpipe called the the voice box. Cords in the voice box are pulled taut by muscles. As the air passes by them, the cords vibrate and make sounds. We make the sounds into words by moving our lips and tongues. See what different shapes you make to say your name.

Food and Digestion

We get our energy from the food we eat. The body uses food as fuel. Like gas in a motor car it has to be 'burned', combined with oxygen, before it can make energy. First it is digested. This means that it is broken down into smaller and smaller bits as it goes from our mouths, through our stomachs to our intestines. The blood collects the food from the intestines and carries it around the body.

Blood

The blood is the body's transport system. It carries oxygen and digested food to all the hungry cells of the body. It carries waste from the cells back to the

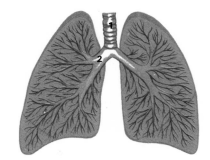

Air passes into the lungs through the trachea (1) and the branching bronchi (2).

lungs and to the kidneys. The blood is pumped round the body by the heart. Nearly 5 quarts of blood are pumped by the heart every minute. You can feel the blood moving when you feel the pulse in your wrist.

Brain and Nerves

The brain is the body's control center. It is connected to every part of the body by nerves. Messages are carried to and from the brain by the nerves. If it gets too dark for you to read this page, nerves from your eyes will inform your brain and the brain will instruct other nerves to tell your muscles to move so that you can put the light on.

Different parts of the brain control different things such as speaking, hearing and seeing. We use our brains to think, and also to 'store' everything that we know.

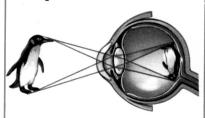

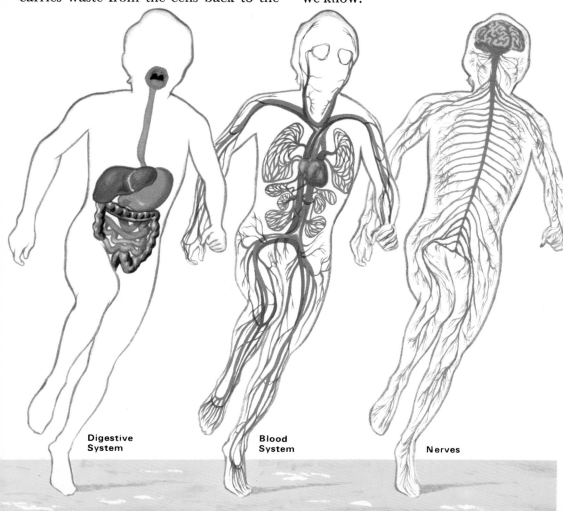

Digestive System   Blood System   Nerves

Food from the Soil

The number of people that can live on the earth depends on the amount of food that can be grown. To provide food, more people work on the land than at anything else. They are able to grow enough to feed over 5,000 million people.

Everywhere in the world, men till the soil and raise animals for food. Our meat comes mainly from cows, pigs, chickens and sheep.

Less than a hundred different plants account for nearly all the food grown on the land. The most important of all crops are the cereals. Wheat, rice, maize, barley, rye and millet give over half of the world's total food supply. Hundreds of millions of tons of these are produced each year.

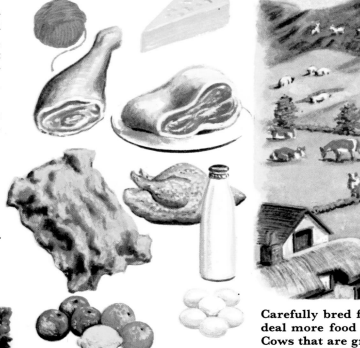

Carefully bred farm animals give a great deal more food than their wild ancestors. Cows that are grazed on the best pastures and that are protected from diseases may give more than 4,500 quarts of milk a year.

Beehives are often placed in an orchard. The bees gather nectar from the blossoms and store it as honey in their hives.

Irrigation has made it possible to farm in even the driest areas. Nearly half the world's farmland is irrigated in some way. Here, a web of ditches brings water to thirsty crops. Below: Using tractors, farmers cultivate vast areas of land.

Where water from wells or springs bubbles to the surface, even the parched desert can be made to bloom. Below: greenhouses trap the sun's heat. In them fruits and vegetables can be grown all year round.

In large farms helicopters are used to spray crops with insecticides. Many different kinds of diseases and pests can attack crops.

Even the steep slopes of a river valley can be cultivated. Grapes are grown in long terraced rows facing the sun. After the grapes are picked, they are pressed and fermented to make wine.

Many tropical fruits and vegetables are grown on plantations. From top to bottom, workers pick coffee, tea and cocoa. Below: Rice, along with wheat, is the world's most important crop. It is grown in specially flooded fields, called paddies.

Left, top to bottom: Some simple farming tools – flail, pitchfork, hoe, rake, scythe and sickle.
A simple plow.
A wind-driven water pump.
A water-wheel used to work a mill.

Better Plants

Through careful breeding, farmers to-day can raise more food than ever before. Food scientists have found special kinds of plants that grow faster and are more hardy. Some kinds of wheat give five times as much grain as their wild ancestors. There are kinds of rice that grow so quickly that several crops can be raised where only one grew in the past.

More Meat, Milk and Eggs

Men have bred domestic animals in the same way they have plants. Animals have long been grazed in special pastures or raised in pens where the food was especially rich and plentiful. Here they could also be protected from diseases and harmful insects.

Over the years, those animals that gave the highest quality meat, milk and eggs were picked out for breeding. With time, new varieties of animals arose. These were far healthier and gave more food of a better quality.

Farming with Machines

Machines are taking the place of animals as 'beasts of burden' on farms. In fact, there are so many machines on a modern farm that the farmworker has to know quite a lot about machinery. Tractors are used for pulling all sorts of things – plows, drills, and harvesters.

The *combine harvester* is a huge machine that cuts the crop and separates the straw and chaff.

Not all the wild creatures that live around farms are a threat to the crops. The millions of tiny creatures that live in the soil are needed to keep it rich and fertile. They help to decompose dead animals and plants into substances the crops use when growing. Some kinds of bacteria live on the roots of plants. Worms help to turn and loosen the soil with their constant tunnelling. Small rodents and many kinds of birds feed on insects that attack the crops.

Preserving Food

Leave a piece of meat or fish around for a few days. It will begin to go bad and start to smell. Leave a piece of bread in the open and it will grow a green mold. Why does this happen? It happens because the air is full of tiny living microbes. These microbes settle on the food and begin to break it down. There are also chemical changes inside the food. The food starts to go bad.

Fortunately we have ways of keeping food fresh. We can *preserve* it in several ways. The first way that our ancestors found out about, long, long ago, was to cook the food. If they cooked meat they could keep it for some time before it went bad. The cooking killed off the microbes that were already in the meat.

Then our ancestors found out about drying food. They hung meat, fish and fruit in the sun until all the water in the food had dried out. Dried food kept for quite a long time because microbes need water to grow. Can you think of some dried foods? Do you know what raisins and prunes are?

Cold is also a very useful way of keeping food fresh. In an ordinary refrigerator we can keep things like milk and meat for a week. In a freezer, where the meat is frozen solid, it can be kept for many months. A huge mammoth that was frozen into solid ice 50,000 years ago in Siberia has been thawed out and eaten. Freezing stops the microbes from growing.

Killing Germs by Heat

Louis Pasteur was one of the greatest Frenchmen who ever lived. He showed that microbes could be killed by heat. Pasteur looked at a drop of milk through a microscope and found that it was full

of microbes. Then he heated the milk and cooled it quickly. Most of the microbes were dead (see pictures above). Today, most of our milk is heated and cooled in this way — it is *pasteurized*. It is safe for us to drink.

Different Food, Different Ways to Keep it Fresh

We can now eat the same things for most of the year. This is because we can preserve food in different ways. Look at the picture above and think how each of the foods can be preserved.

Fruit and vegetables can be shipped long distances in refrigerated ships, railroad cars and trucks. But different fruits have to be kept at different temperatures if they are to stay fresh. Milk can be dried until it becomes a powder. It can then be turned back into liquid milk by adding water to the powder. Bacon can be smoked and salted. Salt is often used to keep fish and meat fresh for some time. It stops the growth of microbes.

Canning

Canning is the most important way of preserving food. Cans are made of thin steel. The steel is coated on both sides with tin. After the food is put in the can, the lid is sealed on as you can see on the right. A machine puts a sealing strip between the lid and the can. Then it presses them tightly together. No air can get into the can.

All the cans are then heated to kill off any germs that would make the food go bad.

As the can is airtight, no live germs can get at the food. So it stays fresh for years.

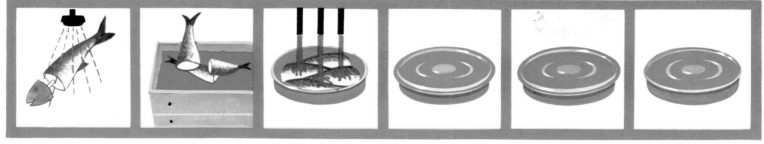

| The fish are cut and washed | They are soaked in salt water | Sometimes sauce is added | Can half sealed as 2 above | Air is driven out by heat | Can is sealed and heated |

Pickling

For many years, fish has been preserved by pickling in brine. (Strong salty water.) Food lasts for quite a long time after being pickled, but it changes its flavor. Most of the 'pickles' we eat have been pickled in vinegar. The pictures below show how fish is pickled in barrels.

| The fish are cleaned | Soaked in brine (salt water) | They are packed in a barrel | Brine is poured into barrel | More fish are added to barrel | Lid of barrel is closed |

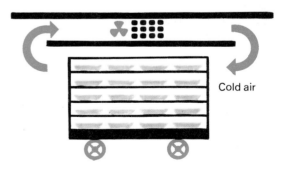

Cold air

Smoking

Fish and meat — especially ham — are preserved by smoking. Herring, salmon and haddock are hung over slow-burning wood fires. The heat of the fire and the chemicals in the wood smoke preserve the fish. They also give the fish a different flavor. Smoked herrings are called 'kippers'. Fish and meat are often dried before being smoked.

Freezing

It has been known for a long time that freezing keeps food from going bad. Fish still goes from the ship to the shop packed in ice.

But most food that has to be kept for a while is now *quick-frozen*. The food is put in a special cold room. There

fans blow a steady blast of very cold air over the food. (See the picture above.) It is frozen very quickly. Then it has to be kept frozen until it is used in your kitchen.

If the food is not frozen very quickly, its flavor and texture are harmed. This is because slow freezing allows big ice crystals to form inside the food. Usually the food is packaged before it is frozen.

Telling the Time

Long before there were clocks and watches people knew roughly what time of day it was. They watched the sun move across the sky. When it was over-head, the day was about half gone. They watched the shadows move with the sun. Then someone had the idea of sticking a piece of wood into the ground. The stick's shadow always moved at the same speed. So the shadow could be used to tell the time of day. This was a simple sundial. A much later sundial is shown opposite (1).

Water and Sand Time

There were other early ways of telling the time. A simple water clock was only a bucket with small holes in the bottom (2). As the water dripped away, and the bucket emptied, people could tell the time by seeing when the water reached lines round the inside.

You have probably seen an egg-timer with sand in it. People used to have big-ger versions of egg-timers called hour

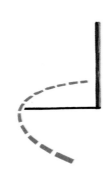

Long, long ago, people used the sun to tell the time. A stick in the ground threw a shadow. The shadow moved around the stick as the sun went across the sky. The shadow told the time of day.

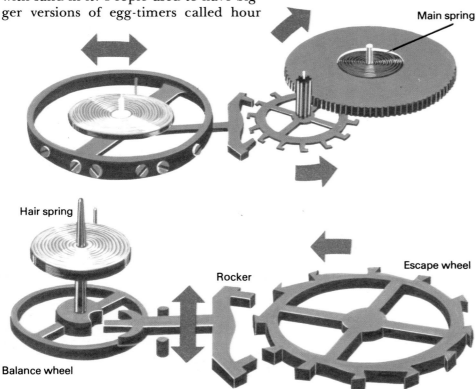

Main spring

Hair spring

Rocker

Escape wheel

Balance wheel

What Makes Time Tick?

In all spring clocks and watches something is needed to make the wheels turn slowly and steadily. In watches and small clocks there is no pendulum. Instead there is a small hair spring. The hair spring makes a balance wheel turn one way, then the other, backwards and forwards. As the balance wheel goes back and forward it moves a rocker with two hooks on it. These hooks catch the teeth in a wheel called the escape wheel and make the clock tick.

They make the escape wheel turn one tooth at a time at a steady speed — always in the same direct-ion. The escape wheel turns the hands of the clock. The top pic-ture shows how the main spring gives the energy to work the escapement. The main spring is the one we wind up.

The Most Famous Clock

The clock that looks down on the Houses of Parliament in London is the most famous clock in the world. During the dark days of World War II its great bell, Big Ben, rang out on radio all over the world to let people know that Britain was still free. The hour bell of the clock weighs $13\frac{1}{2}$ tons. Its huge pendulum is 13 feet long. The working parts of the clock are 16 feet long and $6\frac{1}{2}$ feet wide.

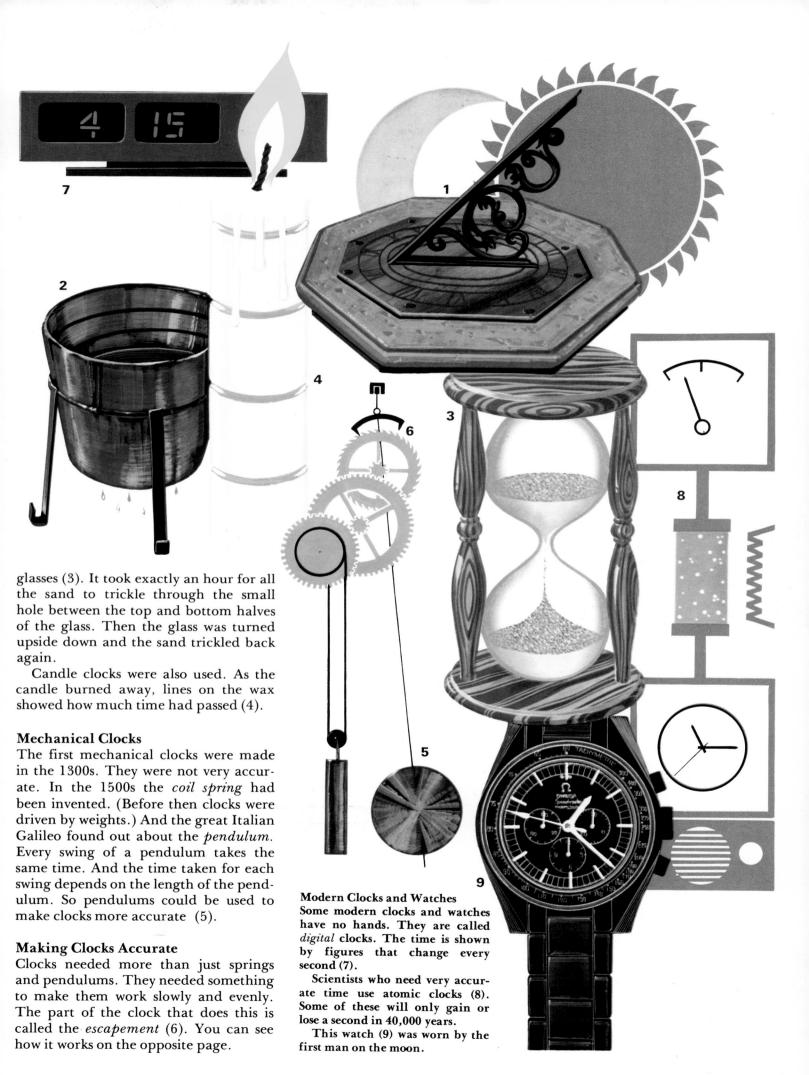

glasses (3). It took exactly an hour for all the sand to trickle through the small hole between the top and bottom halves of the glass. Then the glass was turned upside down and the sand trickled back again.

Candle clocks were also used. As the candle burned away, lines on the wax showed how much time had passed (4).

Mechanical Clocks

The first mechanical clocks were made in the 1300s. They were not very accurate. In the 1500s the *coil spring* had been invented. (Before then clocks were driven by weights.) And the great Italian Galileo found out about the *pendulum*. Every swing of a pendulum takes the same time. And the time taken for each swing depends on the length of the pendulum. So pendulums could be used to make clocks more accurate (5).

Making Clocks Accurate

Clocks needed more than just springs and pendulums. They needed something to make them work slowly and evenly. The part of the clock that does this is called the *escapement* (6). You can see how it works on the opposite page.

Modern Clocks and Watches

Some modern clocks and watches have no hands. They are called *digital* clocks. The time is shown by figures that change every second (7).

Scientists who need very accurate time use atomic clocks (8). Some of these will only gain or lose a second in 40,000 years.

This watch (9) was worn by the first man on the moon.

Making Things Look Bigger

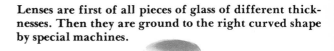

Lenses are used to make things look larger or smaller. They do this by bringing together or spreading out light rays that go through them. Most lenses are made of glass. They are used in things like spectacles, cameras, microscopes, binoculars and telescopes.

How Lenses Work
Lenses work because of their shape. Look closely at a magnifying glass and a pane of ordinary window glass. The window glass is quite flat on both sides. We see things through it just as they are. The magnifying glass is curved slightly on both sides. It makes things look bigger. It is the curve in the magnifying glass that makes it a lens.

The Camera's Lens
Every camera has a lens in it. The lens draws together the light rays as they come into the camera. If we want to take a picture of the candle below we adjust the camera until there is a sharp image of it on the film at the back of the camera. The image of the candle is upside down, but this doesn't matter. It is upside down because light travels in straight lines through the lens, as you can see in the picture.

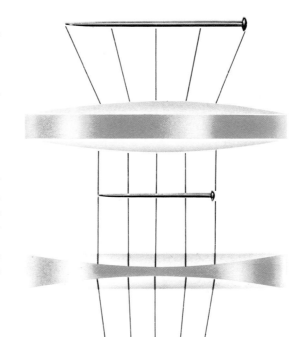

Different Kinds of Lenses
There are different kinds of lenses. Each kind has a different job to do. *Convex* lenses are thicker in the middle than at the edges. When light rays shine through a convex lens they are drawn together so that they meet at a point. A magnifying glass is a lens of this kind.

Concave lenses are thinner in the middle and thicker at the edges. They spread light rays out. If you look through one, things look smaller.

In the picture on the left, the middle pin looks bigger if looked at through the top convex lens. It looks smaller through the bottom concave lens.

Catching Light from the Stars
One of the most important uses for lenses is in telescopes. Big telescopes like the one below are used to collect light from distant stars. A large convex lens at one end of the tube gathers the light from the star. This light is magnified in the eyepiece at the other end.

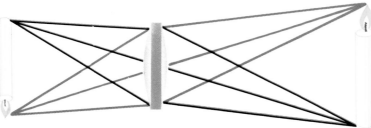

Danger in a Broken Bottle
We know it is dangerous to leave broken bottles lying about. But there is a hidden danger, too. The bottle can behave like a magnifying glass and set fire to grass. Forest fires have started in this way.

Lighthouse Lenses
Lighthouses have to throw a beam of light as far as possible. To do this, a powerful light is shone through many lenses joined together like the ones below.

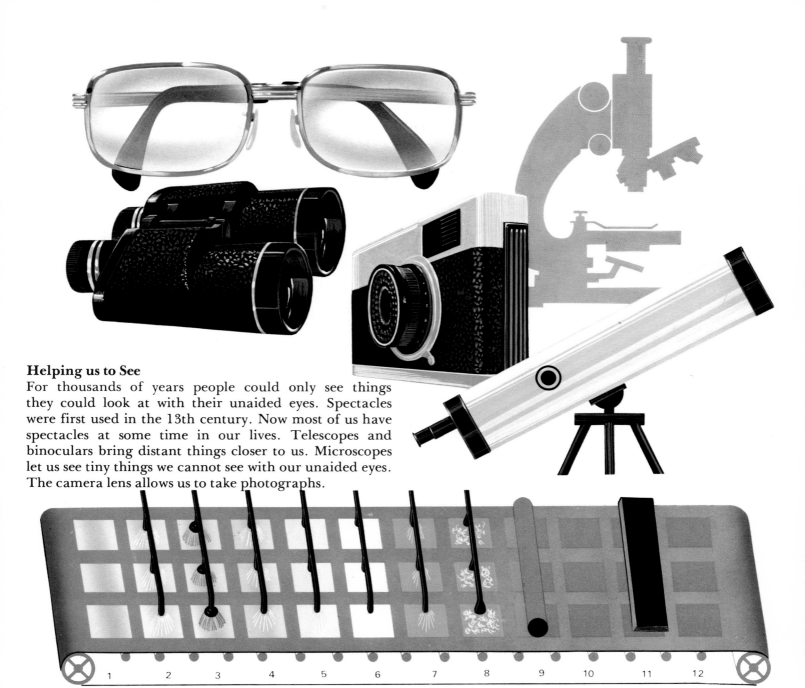

Helping us to See

For thousands of years people could only see things they could look at with their unaided eyes. Spectacles were first used in the 13th century. Now most of us have spectacles at some time in our lives. Telescopes and binoculars bring distant things closer to us. Microscopes let us see tiny things we cannot see with our unaided eyes. The camera lens allows us to take photographs.

Mirrors

A mirror is a piece of glass that has been coated on the back with a film of silver. The picture above shows how mirrors are made. The sheets of glass (1) are washed with ammonia (2), rubbed smooth (3), rinsed with water (4) and given a coat of adhesive (5). Then they are sprayed with silver (6), given a coat of copper (7) and dried by hot air (8). A roller paints the backs of the mirrors (9 and 10). The paint is dried by heat (11). The finished face-down mirrors are shown at (12).

Useful Mirrors

Mirrors, like lenses, can make things look bigger or smaller. The driving mirror (below, left) curves outwards in the middle. It gathers light from a wide area and lets the driver see the whole road behind him. The shaving mirror (below) curves inwards. It makes things bigger.

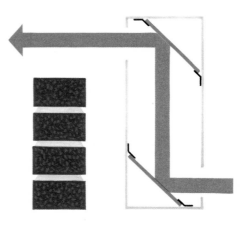

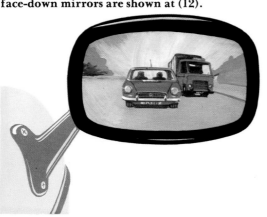

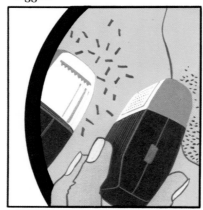

Seeing Round Corners

A submarine puts up a periscope so that the captain can see ships on the surface of the sea. You can make a simple periscope by fixing two mirrors in a cardboard tube. The angle of the mirrors must be the same as in the picture above. Look in the bottom mirror and you can see over a wall.

All Kinds of Glass

Glass is all around us. Think of the things we make from it — windows, bottles, mirrors, light bulbs, drinking glasses, spectacles. And glass can be beautiful, too. It can be colored and made into stained glass windows; it can be cut like a jewel to make it sparkle.

Yet glass is really quite a simple, cheap stuff. It is made from pure sand, mixed with soda and limestone. The mixture is heated until it is a thick, sticky liquid. Then it can be made into almost any shape we want. When it cools it becomes the hard stuff we call glass.

Glass was first made about 4,000 years ago by the Egyptians and the Syrians. These ancient people found out how to make glass beads and other ornaments.

Sometimes volcanoes pour out molten rock that hardens into glass. There is a whole mountain of glass in Yellowstone National Park, Wyoming. When men first set foot on the moon they found they were walking on tiny glass marbles.

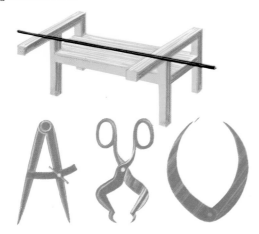

Above you can see some of the tools used by the glassblower. The blow-pipe rests on the glass-blower's 'chair'. He rolls the pipe along the arms of the chair to keep the molten glass in shape. The other tools are for measuring and shaping. The blow-pipe, which is nearly 7 feet long, was invented about 2,000 years ago.

This English glass was made in the 18th century. The pattern in its stem is made by bubbles of air trapped in the glass.

How Glass is Made

The right amounts of sand, lime and soda are mixed. Some broken glass, called 'cullet', is added to speed up the melting. The mixture is heated in a huge furnace.

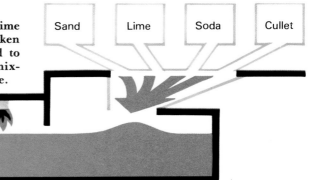

Old Window Glass

Until the 1800s, flat sheets of glass for windows were made by the *crown* process. A round bubble of glass was blown. The end was cut off and it was spun until it was a flat sheet. The sheet was cut into small window panes.

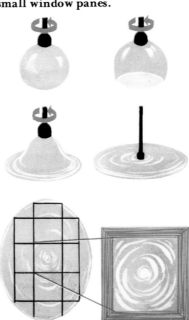

This beautiful wine glass was made in Venice. From the 13th century, Venice was the main glassmaking city in the world.

Blowing Glass

The glassblower takes a blob of molten glass on the end of the blowpipe (1). As he blows through the tube, the glass inflates (2). He turns the pipe and shapes the glass by rolling it (3 and 4). Another rod is attached to the other end of the glass, and the blowpipe is cut off (5). The glass is cut and shaped (6).

For about 1500 years men have shaped glass by blowing through tubes. This is a Medieval glass blower.

Modern Window Glass

Molten glass, like thick, sticky toffee, flows between rollers (left). The flat sheet of glass is carried along on other rollers (below). The glass is slowly cooled. When it is hard it is ground smooth and polished. This is called *plate glass*.

Float Glass

Window glass can also be made by what is called the *float process*. Red hot molten glass is floated on a bath of liquid tin (below). As the glass flows along it becomes very flat and smooth. It does not need to be ground and polished.

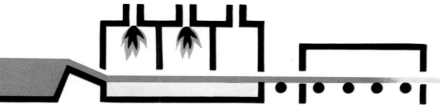

Keeping Warm with Glass

Glass can be made into very fine threads. It is then called *fiberglass.* Fiberglass can be pressed into thick rolls of material. This is used in the roofs of houses to keep the warm air in (below).

Keeping Heat In and Out

A Thermos bottle keeps things hot or cold. It has inside it a glass bottle with double walls. The space between the walls has had all the air pumped out of it. There is no air, so heat has difficulty crossing the space between the glass walls.

Double Glazing

Double glazing is used to keep houses warm. Two layers of glass trap air between them. This undisturbed air allows little heat to cross between the two panes of glass. So less heat is lost from the house than with ordinary windows.

Making Light Bulbs

Early light bulbs like the one invented by Edison (below) had to be blown by men with blowpipes. Nowadays one machine can make 2,000 bulbs every minute. A flowing ribbon of molten glass sags through holes into molds (bottom). Blasts of air force the glass to fill the shape of the molds. Then the molds separate, leaving a chain of light bulbs.

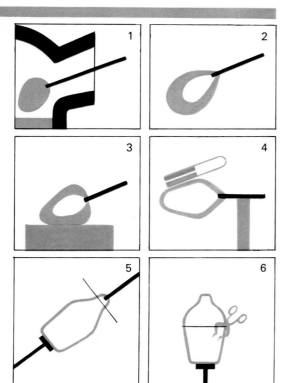

Stained Glass

When a stained glass window is being made, small pieces of glass are fitted together like a jigsaw puzzle. The artist paints on the glass with colored enamel paints. Then the glass is fired in an oven and the enamel becomes part of the glass. The glass jigsaw is held together by lead strips.

From Fibers to Cloth

Most of the clothes we wear are made from thin threads — *fibers.* These threads are twisted together to make longer, stronger lengths of yarn. This twisting of threads together is called *spinning.* The long, twisted yarns are then made into cloth by *weaving* **or** *knitting.*

Wool

Most of the world's wool comes from Australia. And Merino sheep like the one shown at 1 below give the heaviest woolly fleece. Perhaps you have seen pictures of a sheep being sheared by men

with electric clippers. Experts can shear a sheep in about a minute.

The wool from the sheep has to be cleaned and combed before it can be spun into wool yarn.

Linen

Linen is made from the stalks of a plant called flax (2). Flax grows in cool, moist climates. It was spun and woven into cloth long before cotton. Ancient Egyptian mummies were wrapped in it. Nowadays it is used mostly for towels and table linen.

Silk

Silk comes from the cocoon (3) of the silkworm (4). The silkworm, which lives on mulberry leaves, is the caterpillar of a large moth. When it is making its cocoon the silk worm spins a very fine thread, winding it round and round until it is about 1,600 feet long.

Much less silk is used today than there used to be. Materials like nylon can be made much more cheaply.

Camel Hair

Some of the finest cloth comes from the hair of two-humped Bactrian camels (5). During winter the camel grows a thick coat. When summer comes, the coat is shed and made into cloth.

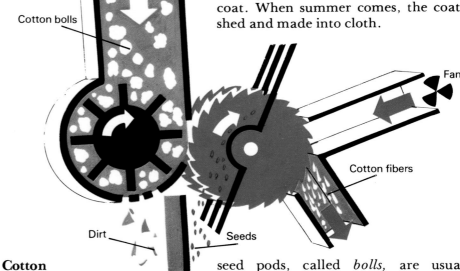

Cotton bolls

Dirt

Seeds

Fan

Cotton fibers

Cotton

Cotton fibers come from the fluffy seed pods of the cotton plant (6). The plant grows in warm countries like the southern states of America and Egypt. Nowadays the seed pods, called *bolls,* are usually picked by big machines. The cotton bolls then go to another machine called a *gin* (above). This machine separates out the fibers from the seed. Other machines clean the fibers and get them ready for spinning into yarn.

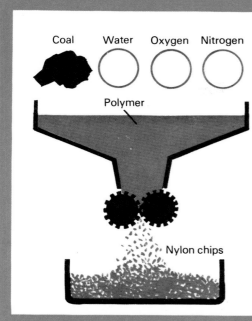

Coal Water Oxygen Nitrogen

Polymer

Nylon chips

Cloth from Chemicals

Today, most of our clothes are made from chemicals. Fibers are made by mixing chemicals into plastics called polymers. Then the polymers are turned into long threads. Nylon is one of these *synthetic fibers.* It can be made from coal and other chemicals as you can see on the left and right. The chemicals are turned into nylon chips. These chips are melted and the liquid nylon is forced through very small holes. This makes long threads which are hardened by a blast of cool air. The threads are wound onto a reel. Then they can be made into cloth, just like cotton.

Synthetic fibers are stronger than natural fibers. They wear better, are waterproof and do not crease as easily. But they are difficult to dye.

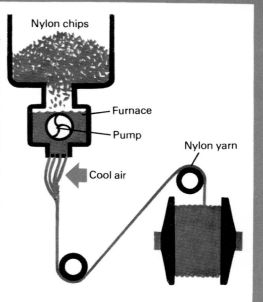

Nylon chips

Furnace

Pump

Nylon yarn

Cool air

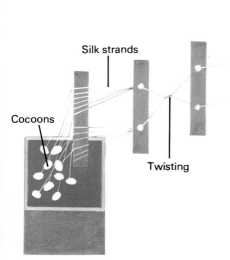

Silk strands

Cocoons

Twisting

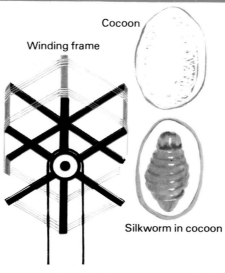

Cocoon

Winding frame

Silkworm in cocoon

RAW MATERIAL

CARDING

COMBING

ROVING

SPINNING

Unwinding the Silk Cocoon

We saw on the opposite page how silk comes from the cocoon of the silkworm. Unraveling this very fine thread from the cocoon is a delicate job. The cocoons

are placed in hot water to melt the gum that holds the threads together. Then the threads from several cocoons are pulled out together and twisted. The silk is wound on a frame.

If we look at woolen yarn through a microscope, we see that the fibers are all tangled up (above).

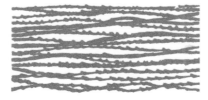

Only man-made fibers and silk have long, continuous strands like those above.

To make what is called *worsted* yarn, the wool fibers are combed and straightened (above). Worsted cloth is stronger and shinier than ordinary woolen cloth.

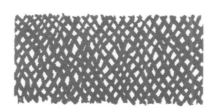

Natural fibers like cotton and wool are made up of short strands, all twisted like those above.

How a Fiber is Made into Strands

The rough cotton or wool has to be made ready for spinning. First it goes through a *carding machine.* This straightens the fibers out and gets rid of the shortest strands. The fibers are then combed by another machine before they go through a roving machine. It pulls the fiber through rollers into finer yarns. They are ready to be spun.

Simple Machines

If you try to lift an automobile you can't. But if you put a jack under one side and turn the jack handle, the car rises. The jack is a simple machine that uses the screw (2) to lift things easily. Anything which uses energy to advantage is a machine.

Six Very Simple Machines

The six things shown in the picture on the right are the simplest possible machines. You may not realize it, but you see some of them every day.

The *wedge* (1) is used to split or pierce things. If we put a wedge in a crack in a piece of wood and hit the wedge with a hammer, the wood will split apart. The wedge being forced into the crack gives a huge outward push in the direction of the black arrows. Chisels, knives and axes are all kinds of wedges.

There are many kinds of *levers* (3). The long piece of wood is a lever. It allows us to move a heavy rock because the distance between A and B is shorter than the distance between B and C. We could not lift the rock without a lever.

The picture at 4 shows an *inclined plane* (a slope). Pulling a heavy load up the slope takes less effort than lifting it straight up from the ground.

The *pulley* (5) is another way of lifting heavy loads easily. The *wheel and axle* (6) allows us to move things along the ground much more easily than by dragging them.

Scientists say that work is done when a force moves something. When you pull or lift something, you are doing work. *Power* is the rate at which work is done. Scientists measure power in things called *watts*. A small electric heater uses electricity at the rate of 1000 watts (1 kilowatt). One horsepower equals 746 watts, so a horse pulling as hard as it could, would not keep a small electric heater going.

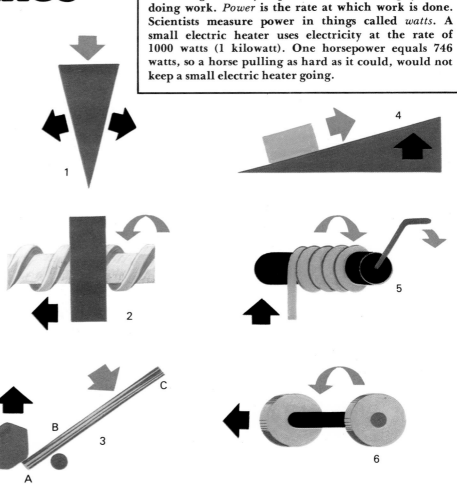

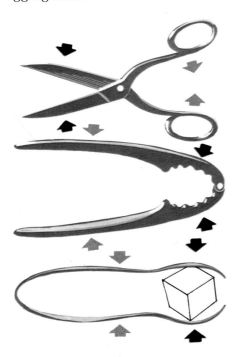

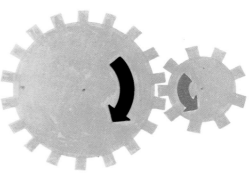

There are many kinds of levers, some of which we use every day. Scissors are levers. They let us use a lot of cutting power without much effort. Nutcrackers (center far left) are even more powerful levers. A small squeeze at the handle end becomes a large force at the jaws. But the leverage of sugar tongs (bottom far left) is not strong. Can you think why?

The picture on the left shows a *block and tackle*. It is used to lift heavy weights. The more wheels that are used, the easier the lifting is.

Gears (above) are simple machines that change speed and help to do work. If the small wheel with 9 teeth turns once, the big wheel with 18 teeth makes only half a turn. But the turning force of the big wheel is twice that of the small one.

When we pull a nail out of wood like this we are using a lever. It makes the job much easier.

A chisel is also a simple lever, rather like the wedge.

The screw is really a kind of inclined plane. As it turns round and round, the spirals (the *thread*) of the screw pull it into the wood.

The can-opener is another kind of lever. The force at the cutting tip of the opener is much greater than the force you use on the handle.

A *crowbar* can be used for opening cases. It is a simple lever. The longer the handle, the more force you have at the working end.

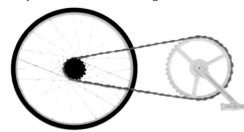

One turn of the big bicycle gear makes the small gear, and the whole wheel, go round quickly. That is why bicycles can travel fast.

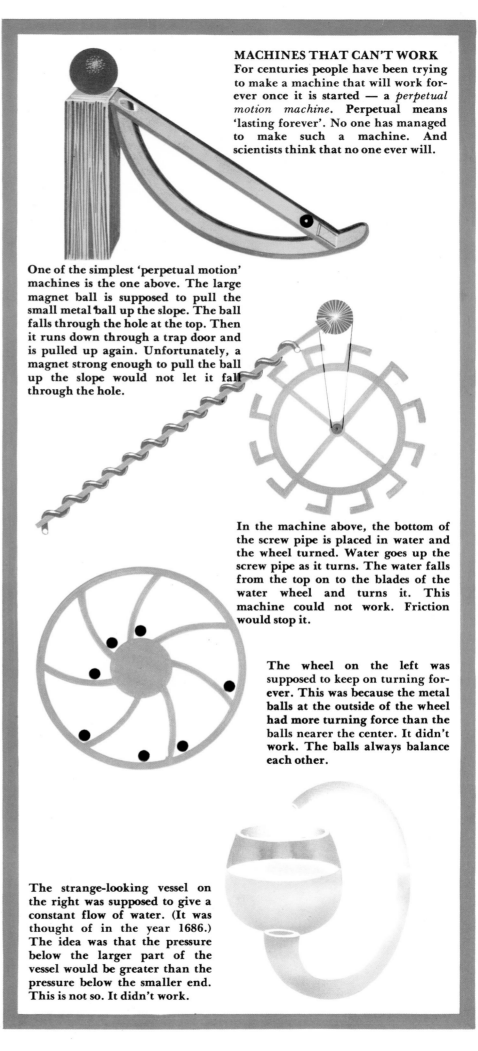

MACHINES THAT CAN'T WORK

For centuries people have been trying to make a machine that will work forever once it is started — a *perpetual motion machine*. Perpetual means 'lasting forever'. No one has managed to make such a machine. And scientists think that no one ever will.

One of the simplest 'perpetual motion' machines is the one above. The large magnet ball is supposed to pull the small metal ball up the slope. The ball falls through the hole at the top. Then it runs down through a trap door and is pulled up again. Unfortunately, a magnet strong enough to pull the ball up the slope would not let it fall through the hole.

In the machine above, the bottom of the screw pipe is placed in water and the wheel turned. Water goes up the screw pipe as it turns. The water falls from the top on to the blades of the water wheel and turns it. This machine could not work. Friction would stop it.

The wheel on the left was supposed to keep on turning forever. This was because the metal balls at the outside of the wheel had more turning force than the balls nearer the center. It didn't work. The balls always balance each other.

The strange-looking vessel on the right was supposed to give a constant flow of water. (It was thought of in the year 1686.) The idea was that the pressure below the larger part of the vessel would be greater than the pressure below the smaller end. This is not so. It didn't work.

Radio

Wherever you are there are almost certainly radio waves passing all around you and through you. These waves travel very fast indeed — at the speed of light. In a broadcasting station, sound waves from a person's voice are turned into radio waves. These waves travel through the air to your radio. The radio turns them back into sound waves that you can hear.

Radio is important, not only in giving us information and entertainment. It is a very useful form of communication between ships and shore stations, and between aircraft and control towers at airports.

How Radio Began

It is difficult to say who invented radio. But the German scientist Heinrich Hertz was probably the first man to make radio waves — in 1888.

The man who made radio really work was an Italian, Guglielmo Marconi. Marconi had an Irish mother and he did most of his work in England. In 1899 he sent the first radio signal across the English Channel. Then in 1901 he astonished everyone by sending a signal right across the Atlantic Ocean — a distance of about 2,000 miles. The signal was the letter S in the Morse Code — dot-dot-dot.

Marconi used electric sparks to send out his radio signals. All that could be heard at the receiving end was a buzzing sound. This buzzing could be broken up into the dots and dashes of the Morse Code.

The next step in the story of radio was the sending out of the human voice. This became possible when the radio valve was invented in the early 1900s.

Today, people all over the world can speak to each other by radio. Scientists even send radio signals out into space in the hope that they will be heard and understood by people on some very distant planet.

And, of course, radio waves carry the sounds and pictures for our television programs.

How Does Radio Work?

In the broadcasting studio someone sings into a microphone. The microphone changes the sound waves made by the person's voice into electrical waves running along wires. These electrical waves are strengthened (amplified) in the control room.

At the same time another, much stronger, electrical wave is made to run through wires at the transmitter. This is called the *carrier wave*.

The waves from the person's voice are added on to the carrier wave. And these joined up electrical waves are sent along a wire to the transmitting (sending out) aerial. From the aerial, radio waves go out in all directions.

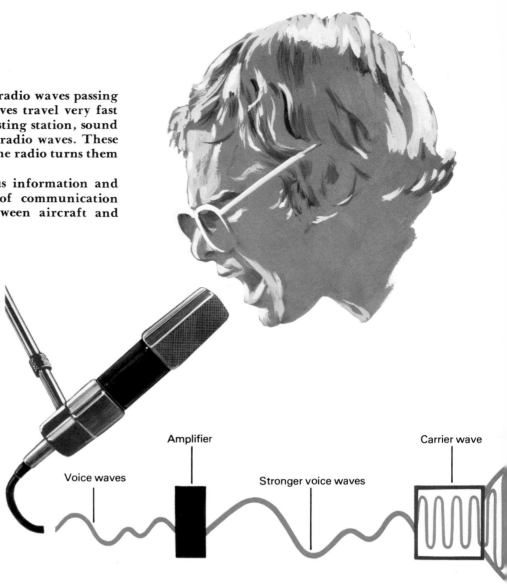

Voice waves   Amplifier   Stronger voice waves   Carrier wave

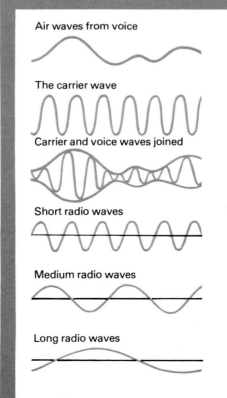

Air waves from voice

The carrier wave

Carrier and voice waves joined

Short radio waves

Medium radio waves

Long radio waves

All Kinds of Waves

Radio waves, light waves and heat waves all shoot out at the same speed — 186,300 miles a second. Scientists think nothing can travel faster than these mysterious waves. (Ordinary sound waves from your voice or a musical instrument go through the air much more slowly — at only 1,115 feet a second.)

Radio waves are quite invisible to us. But we know that the lengths of the waves are all different. (The wavelength is the distance from the top of one hump to the top of the next.) Some radio waves are very short — only a few inches long. Others are very long — over 6,500 feet from wave to wave.

Ordinary voice waves need air to travel through. Radio waves do not need air. That is why we can talk by radio to astronauts on the moon. The radio waves between earth and the moon have traveled through space where there is no air.

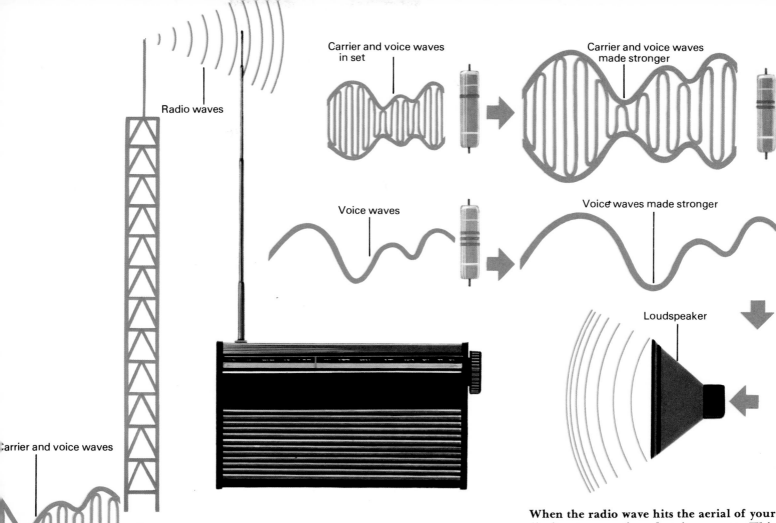

Radio waves

Carrier and voice waves in set

Carrier and voice waves made stronger

Voice waves

Voice waves made stronger

Loudspeaker

Carrier and voice waves

Bouncing Radio Waves

Radio waves travel in straight lines. Why then can radios out of sight of the transmitting aerial pick up the waves? They do this because radio waves can bounce off things, just as light waves are bounced off a mirror. Some waves go along the ground, but they cannot be used over long distances because the earth is curved.

Other waves shoot upwards

until they hit a band of air called the *ionosphere.* From this special band of air they are bounced back to earth. The radio waves can go on bouncing up and down all the way round the earth.

When the radio wave hits the aerial of your radio it sets up a tiny electric current. This current carries the waves of the carrier and the microphone waves from the person's voice. When the radio is tuned to the wavelength of the radio waves they pass into the radio. There they are made stronger.

The radio then takes away the carrier wave and leaves the electrical waves made by the person's voice in the microphone. These waves are again increased in strength and go along wires to the loudspeaker. The loudspeaker behaves like a microphone in reverse. The electrical waves make it vibrate and make sound waves in the air. The sound waves are the same as those made by the person singing into the microphone.

And all this happens in a flash.

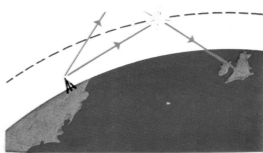

Not all radio waves bounce back from the ionosphere. Some very short waves such as those used for television go straight through and disappear into space. If we want to send television pictures across the Atlantic, we have to bounce them back to earth from a special satellite high up over the ocean.

A Morse key

The Morse Code

In the early days of radio all messages were sent by Morse Code. This code was invented by the American Samuel Morse and the International Morse Code (below) is still used.

```
A ·—          P ·——·
B —···         Q ——·—
C —·—·         R ·—·
D —··          S ···
E ·            T —
F ··—·         U ··—
G ——·          V ···—
H ····         W ·——
I ··           X —··—
J ·———         Y —·——
K —·—          Z ——··
L ·—··
M ——
N —·
O ———
```

Television

Television works a lot like radio. It uses radio waves to bring pictures and sound from one place to another without using wires. It lets us see things on the other side of the world at the same instant they are happening.

How Television Works

The pictures begin when a special camera photographs a scene. The cameraman in the television studio aims his camera at a newscaster. The newscaster's picture is picked up by the camera and turned into electrical waves. These waves are transmitted as radio waves. Your TV set receives the radio waves and turns them back into a picture.

Like a film, a TV program is split up into a lot of still pictures. These still pictures follow each other so quickly — about 25 every second — our eyes see a moving scene.

The newscaster's picture in the TV camera is split up into its three primary colors of light — red, green and blue. Each light color goes through a special tube inside the camera. These tubes

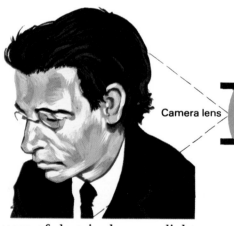

make a pattern of electric charge as light falls on them. A beam of electrons in each tube moves quickly over the pattern of electric charge, going from left to right and top to bottom. This is called *scanning*. It makes a stream of electric signals, each signal telling how bright or dark a tiny part of the picture is.

The whole picture is scanned 25 times every second. So 25 still pictures are sent out a second. And each of these pictures is made up of 625 separate lines that have been scanned. (You can see these lines if you look closely at the screen of your set.)

The electric signals are amplified and sent out from the aerial on top of a high television mast. They are now radio waves.

Camera lens · *Mirrors* · *Filters* · *Sound joined to picture signals* · *Picture signals amplified*

The picture goes through a glass lens into the television camera (above). There it is split up by special mirrors and filters into the three simple light colors, red, green and blue. Each color goes into a separate tube.

The picture below shows one of the three tubes. Inside the tube the light falls on a special plate. This plate turns the picture into dots of electricity. These dots travel to a target screen. An electron gun scans all over the target screen. The reflected beam of electrons is collected and amplified before it goes out to be transmitted as radio waves.

The sound wave carrying the newscaster's voice is added to the carrier wave before it goes out.

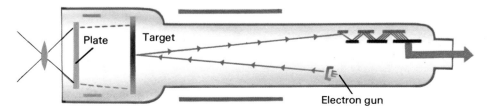

Plate · *Target* · *Electron gun*

Television

The electron beam scans the television screen in a zig-zag. First of all it scans the odd-numbered lines. Then it scans the even-numbered lines, as in the pictures below. There are really 625 lines on the screen. The whole screen is scanned 25 times a second.

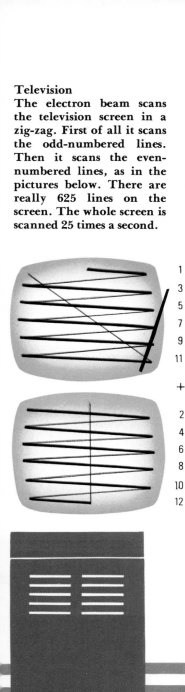

1
3
5
7
9
11

+

2
4
6
8
10
12

Inside Your TV Set

The radio waves from the television transmitting aerial shoot out in all directions. The aerial attached to your TV set is specially shaped to catch the waves. These waves are turned back into electric signals in the aerial. The signals are amplified in the set — they are made stronger — and the picture signals are separated from the sound signal. They are very like the signals that left the camera and microphone in the studio.

Your TV Picture

The picture electric signals go into the *cathode-ray tube* — the large glass tube you may have seen in television sets. It is the front of the cathode-ray tube you look at when you watch TV. An electron gun from each color makes a scanning beam. The scanning beams vary in strength as the picture signals vary. These beams hit a special screen in the front of the cathode-ray tube, making little flashes of colored light where they hit. Some of these tiny flashes are brighter than others as the beams from the electron guns become stronger or weaker.

The Picture is Built Up

The beams travel over the screen line after line, very, very quickly. As they do so they build up the picture in the same way it was broken down in the television camera in the studio. Twenty-five complete pictures are built up every second. So our eyes see a moving scene like that in the TV studio. What we are really seeing is a picture made up of thousands upon thousands of tiny red, green and blue flashes of light.

Inside the TV set the sound signals are separated from the picture signals. They are turned into actual sounds in a loudspeaker, as in a radio.

The color picture is built up by thousands of tiny flashes of red, green and blue light.

Recording Sound

Until the year 1877 no one had ever heard the sound of his own voice as it sounds to other people. In that year the versatile inventor Thomas Edison recited 'Mary had a little lamb' into a tube. At the end of the tube was a thin metal disc that moved back and forth (vibrated) as Edison spoke. A blunt needle was attached to the disc. This vibrating needle cut a wavy groove in a turning drum covered in tinfoil. The wavy groove in the tinfoil was a copy of the loudness and pitch of Edison's voice. When he put a simple horn in the tube and turned the drum again, he could hear a very scratchy voice saying, 'Mary had a little lamb . . .' Edison had discovered a way of recording sound.

The Gramophone

In Edison's 'improved phonograph' the vibrating needle cut a wavy groove in a wax drum. Then the drum was changed to a flat disc, much the same as we use today.

Today's Records

Today, records are made and played back electrically. But we still use a wavy groove and a vibrating needle. Records

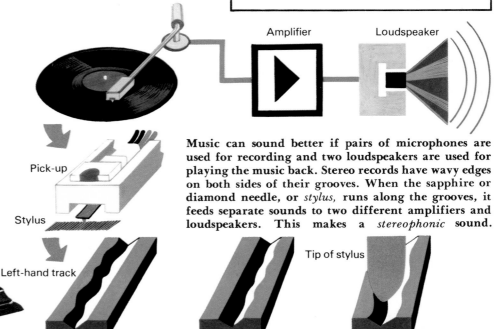

Pick-up

Stylus

Left-hand track

Record groove

Right-hand track

Amplifier Loudspeaker

Music can sound better if pairs of microphones are used for recording and two loudspeakers are used for playing the music back. Stereo records have wavy edges on both sides of their grooves. When the sapphire or diamond needle, or *stylus,* runs along the grooves, it feeds separate sounds to two different amplifiers and loudspeakers. This makes a *stereophonic* sound.

Tip of stylus

Edison's phonograph

are made of hard plastic. By making the grooves very fine, our records play for much longer than they used to. They now go round 33 times a minute, instead of the old 78 times.

How a Record is Made

The sound to be put on record is picked up by a microphone. The microphone turns the sound air waves into electric waves. These electric waves go to a chisel-shaped piece of sapphire. The piece of sapphire is made to vibrate like the original sound. It cuts a very fine wavy groove in a smooth plastic disc. This becomes the 'master' disc.

After the recording is finished, the master disc is sprayed with liquid silver. This is then covered with a thin layer of nickel. When the nickel film is peeled off it has on it the imprint of the grooves of the master disc. Only it has ridges that stick out, instead of grooves.

This disc is used to make another disc like the master, only stronger. And from this disc are made several metal discs called 'stampers'. These discs have ridges that stick out, instead of grooves. They

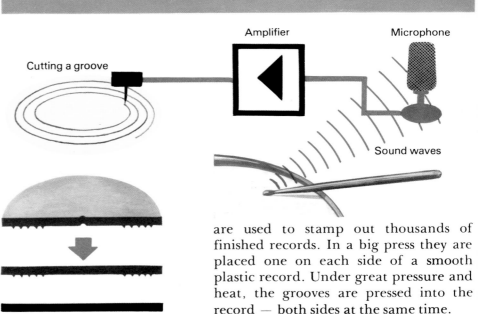

Cutting a groove

Amplifier Microphone

Sound waves

are used to stamp out thousands of finished records. In a big press they are placed one on each side of a smooth plastic record. Under great pressure and heat, the grooves are pressed into the record — both sides at the same time.

A Stereo Record

To make a stereo record, separate tape recordings are made of the sound coming from each side of an orchestra. Both these recordings are cut as wavy lines on either side of the same groove of the disc (see above).

Putting Sound on Tape

In tape recorders a magnet is used to record sound on a long plastic ribbon. The ribbon is coated with tiny magnetic particles. To make a recording, we speak into a microphone. This turns the sound of our voice into electrical signals. These signals are sent through a coil of

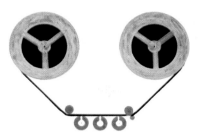

As the tape is wound from one spool to the other, it passes close to the magnets, or *heads*.

Some tape recorders have three heads — one to record, one to play back and one to take away the recording from the tape.

When a recording is being played back, the tape with your voice on it is moved past the playback head. The little magnets in the tape, which carry your words, make a magnetic field in the playback head. This changing magnetic field makes a small electric current in a coil. The current is amplified and made to work a loudspeaker. Your voice comes from the speaker.

Magnetic particles in tape before recording

Magnetic particles after recording

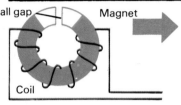

wire wound round a circular magnet. The magnet has a tiny gap in the circle. A magnetic field that varies as your voice does is made across this gap. As the tape winds past the gap, the magnetic particles in the tape are rearranged. They become arranged in an order commanded by the sound of your voice. Your voice is recorded on the tape.

Microphone

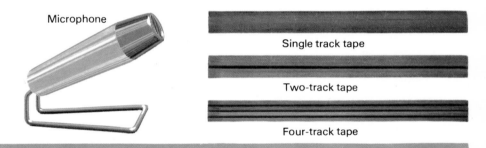

Single track tape

Two-track tape

Four-track tape

Sounds on Film

Another way of recording sound is used for movie films. The films that run through moving picture projectors have what is called a 'sound track' along one edge of the film. (See the picture on the right.) There are two different kinds of sound track, but they both work in nearly the same way. They work by shining light through the edge of the film. The top picture on the right has light and dark bands along the sound track. These bands match the original sound waves. The other piece of film has a wavy black band on its edge. This too matches the original sound waves.

While the film is running, a strong light shines through the sound track. The amount of light getting through the film depends on the pattern on the sound track. More light gets through light areas on the track. This varying pattern of light falls on a *photoelectric cell*. A photo-electric cell is sometimes called an electric eye. When light shines on it, an electric current flows. The strength of

the current depends on how much light shines on it. So you can see that the varying light shining through the sound track can make a varying electric current. This current is amplified and fed to a loudspeaker. We hear the sound. And since the sound is on the same film as the pictures, the sound and pictures should always be in step.

Photoelectric cells have many other uses. They can be much more sensitive to light than the human eye. Doors that open by themselves as you walk towards them are worked by photoelectric cells. A beam of light shines on a cell. When you walk across the beam, the current in the cell is cut off. A special electromagnet that normally pulls two switch contacts apart, allows them to touch. This works a motor that opens the door.

Photoelectric cells set off burglar alarms, turn street lights on and off, measure the amount of light going into a camera and adjust the lens. They are also used in artificial satellites to take power from the sun.

On and In the Sea

Today, very few people travel long distances by sea. Aircraft carry passengers to all parts of the world much more quickly. But we still need cargo ships to carry heavy loads. Taking heavy loads by air would be much too expensive. We cannot do without huge tankers, for instance, to carry cargoes such as oil. And for short distances people travel quickly across the water in hovercraft and hydroplanes.

Learning to Sail

The first boat was probably a floating log. Over thousands of years men found out about rafts and canoes. Then came sailing ships. The wind was the only kind of power at sea for very many years. And, as time went by, the design of sailing ships improved so much the fast clipper ships could reach speeds of up to 23 miles an hour.

The Age of Steam

While the fast clippers were sailing the oceans, men were already trying to fit the new steam engines into ships. The first steamships were driven by huge paddle wheels, either on the sides of the ships or at the stern. But these were not very successful. They wasted a lot of energy just churning up the water.

Then came the propeller and better steam-turbine engines. The great days of the steamship had begun.

Today most cargo ships are powered by diesel engines. And perhaps the ships of the future will be driven by nuclear power, as a few already are. They can stay at sea for very long periods of time without refueling.

Hovercraft are the only craft which can travel over land or water. The one above is a giant SRN4. It is driven by four propellers, just like an aircraft. Air blown out beneath the hovercraft lifts it off the water. Since there is therefore very little friction, the craft can travel very fast.

One of the earliest and simplest kinds of boat was the *coracle* (above). It was made from animal skins sewn together and stretched over a wooden frame.

The war galleys of the Greeks and Romans had two or three banks of oars to speed them along. They also carried a square sail for extra speed when the wind was behind them.

Submarines are very important naval vessels. Because they can travel under water, they are difficult to track down. Submarines have *ballast tanks*. When these tanks are filled with water, the submarine dives. When the water in the tanks is pumped out, the submarine rises to the surface.

Torpedoes are usually the submarine's main weapon. Their propellers are driven by electricity or by steam. The front of the torpedo is full of explosive which goes off when a ship is hit, usually underwater. Some torpedoes can guide themselves toward an enemy ship.

Finding the Depth

Radar cannot be used under water. To find the depth of water under a ship, sailors use *sonar.* Pulses of very high-pitched sound are sent out from the bottom of the ship. The time taken for sound to reach the sea bottom and bounce back to the ship is recorded. The longer it takes, the deeper is the water. As the ship sails along, a chart of the sea bottom is drawn by the sonar machine. The wavy lines at the bottom of the picture show this.

Sonar is also used to find shoals of fish and wrecks on the seabed.

Hydroplanes like the one above 'fly' above the surface of the water. When the boat is not moving, it sits on the water like an ordinary craft. But as it gathers speed it rises out of the water and sits on its underwater wings (hydrofoils). Because there is very little friction between the wings and the water, hydroplanes can travel very fast.

Early steamships were driven by huge paddles (center). But propellers don't waste as much energy. They bite into water in the same way a screw bites into wood. The first propellers were like the one on the right. Now they have four or three blades like that on the left.

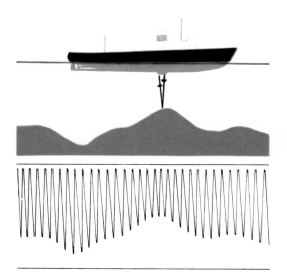

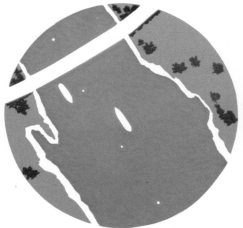 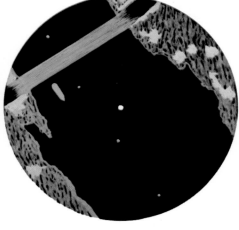

A Dry Dock

When repair work has to be done on ships' bottoms, or rudders, or propellers, the ship has to be put into dry dock.

A dry dock is like a huge concrete box sunk into the ground. One end of the dock opens on to a harbor. Water is allowed to flow into the dock (1 below). Then the huge solid steel gates at the end of the dock are opened and the ship sails in (2).

The gates are closed and the water is pumped out of the dock (3). As the ship sinks with the water it comes to rest on the bottom of the dock. There it is supported by wooden beams between it and the side of the dock.

Then men can go in to carry out whatever repairs are needed underneath the ship.

When the repairs are finished, water is allowed to flow into the dock again until it rises to the same level as the water in the harbor outside. The gates are opened and the ship sails out.

Seeing in the Dark

Radar is a way of finding out how far away things are and their position — things like ships, aircraft or objects on land. It can pick up aircraft hundreds of miles away. And it works in fog or in darkness.

A Radar Picture

The ship in the center of the picture above left uses its radar set. In the chart room the radar screen builds up the picture on the right. The officer on duty can see on the screen another ship approaching and a line of buoys. He can also see the outline of the land on either side. He can see a bridge ahead. Radar tells him exactly where he is.

How Radar Works

A radar set sends out radio waves from a special aerial. When the waves hit something they are bounced back to the radar aerial. The radar set works out how long the waves took to reach the target and come back. It knows how fast radio waves travel. So it can record how far away the target is. The aerial goes round. This lets the radar record the direction of the target.

1

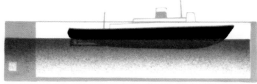

2

3

Railways

Travel by Rail

The time between 1825 and 1900 is sometimes called the Railway Age. In that brief time more than 600,000 miles of railway lines were built all over the

There were railways long before man invented the steam engine. The ancient Greeks discovered that wagons could be pulled much more easily if they ran the wheel along wooden planks. By doing this they cut down friction. But it was not until 1825 that there were railways as we know them. In that year George Stephenson opened the Stockton and Darlington Railway. The engine, *Locomotion No.1*, puffed its way along at 7 miles per hour. The train shown below is on the Japanese Tokaido line. It averages over 105 miles per hour.

world. People could travel long distances in a way they could never do before.

Now the railways are not as important as they used to be. Cars, trucks and aircraft have taken over some of the jobs the railways used to do. But we still need trains to carry freight. Smooth rails are still a cheap way of carrying heavy loads.

Today's Engines

There are two main kinds of engines on the railways today — electric and diesel. Electric engines are driven by electric motors. The electric motors turn the wheels. The electricity is picked up either from an overhead wire or from a third rail.

Diesel engines burn oil as fuel. The power from the diesel engine can be taken to the wheels in different ways. In diesel-electric trains, the diesel engine makes electricity. The electricity goes to electric motors that turn the wheels. Or the diesel engine's power goes through some gears straight to the train's wheels.

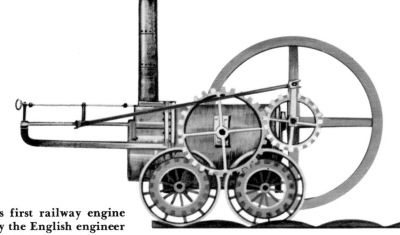

The world's first railway engine was made by the English engineer Richard Trevithic in 1804. It was a strange-looking engine, but it worked. The huge flywheel was needed to help it work smoothly. It only had one large steam cylinder.

In 1879 the world's first electric locomotive (right) was made by the German Werner von Siemens. This strange little engine pulled passengers round a railway line at a Berlin exhibition.

Before the steam engine, mine trucks were pushed along wooden rails. The trucks' wheels had flanges to hold them on the rails.

When the railways first came in, the cars had flat wheels and the rails were L-shaped (above). The cars could be used on ordinary roads.

The modern rail is shaped like the one above. Most of the world's railways have a track in which the rails are 4ft 8½ in (1.435 meters) apart. This is called *standard gauge*.

Hovertrains

Hovercraft glide over land or water on a cushion of air. People are now building hovertrains. The one above is French. It glides over a single rail — a *monorail* track made of concrete. Because there is hardly any friction to slow it down, it goes very fast. This hovertrain is pushed along by a propeller, like an aircraft. It reaches a speed of 233 miles per hour.

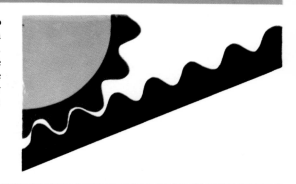

When trains have to climb up mountains, ordinary smooth wheels do not give enough grip. Mountain railways usually have racks like the one in the picture on the right. These racks allow the trains to move up and down safely.

Signals and Points

Train engineers must obey signals. The early signals were worked by hand. The signalman pulled a lever in his cabin and the signals rose or fell. When the signal arm was down, the train could go. These were called *semaphore signals* (right). The bottom signal with the fish-tail end was the *distant* signal. It told the driver what the next *home* signal was reading.

Nowadays, signals are electric. They have colored lights, something like road traffic signals (far right). A red light means stop. A green means all-clear. And a yellow light means that the next signal may be red.

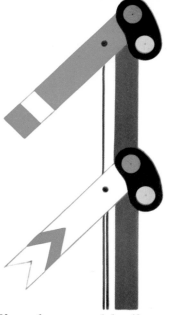

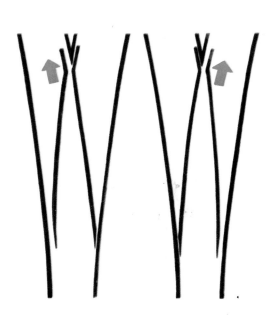

If you have a model railway you will know that to switch a train from one track to another you need *points*. In the old days a man had to stand beside the track and pull a lever to shift the points. Now points are changed electrically from a distant signal box. The picture on the left shows how points work.

Nowadays, signals and points are usually interlocked for safety. The points can only be moved when the correct signal is showing.

The Car

Every year more than a million new cars come on to the roads. Modern cars are quiet, fast and easy to drive. We are so used to them we take them for granted. But the car of today is really quite a wonderful thing. It may have more than 15,000 different parts. And most of these parts keep on working most of the time. But 70 years ago, cars were very rare. They looked very different too. They were noisy and slow, and they broke down often.

Car Facts
The British 'Red Flag Act' of 1865 said that every car had to have a man walking in front of it with a red flag. The maximum speed allowed was 4 mph (6 km/h).
Diesel engines are similar to gasoline engines. They run on cheaper oil fuel and do not need spark plugs. But they have less powerful acceleration.
In 1913, Henry Ford revolutionized the auto industry when his Model T became the first car made from a moving assembly line. Low cost cars became widely available.

Modern sports cars are powerful and fast. Their streamlined shape slices easily through the air.

The First Cars
The first true automobiles came onto the road about 100 years ago. They looked a lot like horseless carriages. The bodies were high and square, like boxes. They were built of wood and metal. The driver and passengers sat on hard seats out in the open. The wheels were either made of wood with an iron rim or from solid rubber. These cars jolted and bounced a lot as they drove along. Yet, all in all, cars worked in much the same way they do today.

Better Cars
At the beginning of the present century cars began to look more as they do today. The engine was usually in front. It ran on a mixture of gas and air. In front of it there was a radiator that kept the engine cool. The car had a spare tire in case of a flat. Inside there was plenty of room for passengers and luggage.

Steering the Car
Cars had to be steered differently from carriages. The axle and front wheels of a horse-drawn carriage turned together round a metal pin (right). But cars needed a steering that was safer. The axle of a car is fixed in one place. It always points forward. Only the wheels are allowed to turn from side to side to turn the car.

The world's first successful car was built by the German Karl Benz in 1885 (below).

Gottlieb Daimler built one of the first gasoline engines. In 1885 he put it on a bicycle and made the world's first motorcycle.

The earliest cars came in every shape and size. Often, old horse-drawn carriages were used for the body of the car.

Steering a carriage   Steering a car

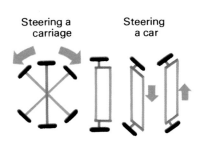

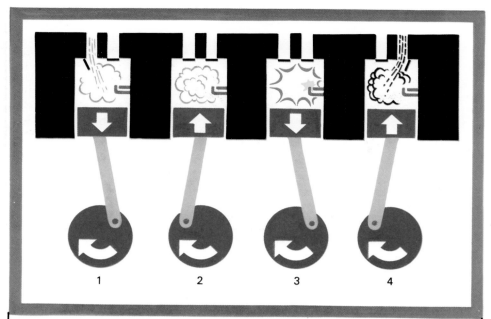

The heart of a car engine is a set of tube-like *cylinders*. Inside each cylinder is a close-fitting plunger called a *piston*. The pistons move up and down inside the cylinders. As each piston travels down, a mixture of gas and air is sprayed into the top of the cylinder (1). This mixture is squeezed as the piston moves back up (2). Then a spark sets the mixture alight. It explodes (3). The piston is pushed down by the explosion. When it comes up again, the piston pushes the leftover gases (the exhaust) out of the cylinder (4). Now the engine is ready to begin at (1) again.

Each time a piston goes up and down it helps turn the crankshaft.

Racing cars can drive for hours at very high speeds. Some have special 'wings' fixed to the back and front. They help to hold the car on the ground. Big fat tires are also needed to hold the road. Some racing cars even have four front wheels for extra speed and better grip (below).

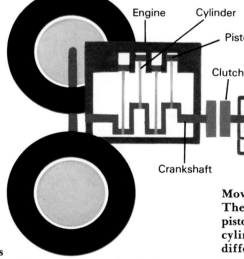

Engine   Cylinder

Piston

Clutch   Gearbox

Propeller shaft

Crankshaft

The Brakes

There are brakes on all four wheels of a car. The driver presses down the brake pedal. The pedal is linked to the *brake shoes.* They are found just inside the turning *wheel drums*. When the pedal is pushed, the brakes are forced apart. They rub on the wheel drums and stop them turning.

In other kinds of brakes, called *disc brakes*, metal discs go round with the car's wheels. When the brake pedal is pressed, pads grip the discs. The car slows down.

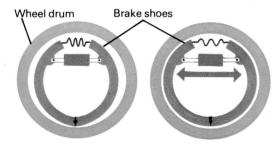

Wheel drum   Brake shoes

Moving the Car

The power of a car begins when the pistons move up and down in the cylinders. Each piston moves at a different time from the others. While one piston goes up, another comes down. Together they turn the crankshaft.

The crankshaft is joined to the *clutch* and the *gearbox.* Most cars have four gears in the gearbox to make them go forward. A driver needs all the power he can get to start moving. He uses first gear. The second and third gears are for increasing speed and climbing hills. When the car is going fast, the driver uses the fourth gear.

The clutch is for cutting off the engine from the gears. When the driver wants to change from one gear to another, he presses down on the clutch pedal. This separates the turning crankshaft from the gears.

The power of the engine goes from the gearbox to a long rod called the *propeller shaft.* The spinning shaft turns the rear axle. As the axle turns it makes the wheels go round. The car goes forward.

The Gears

The gears in a car look like wheels with teeth. Small gear wheels turn faster than big ones. The small wheel below has 8 teeth. It will turn twice as fast as the big wheel with 16 teeth.

In the Air

Our age can certainly be called the Air Age. Airliners like *Concorde* flash across the sky at more than 1240 miles an hour. Great Jumbo jets take off with over 400 passengers on board. Yet, at the beginning of this century no one had flown in an aircraft.

The first of the big jumbo aircraft was the Boeing 747. When it first carried passengers in 1970 it weighed twice as much as any other airliner. Its huge cabin is 20 feet wide and 187 feet long. From wing-tip to wing-tip it measures over 124 feet. And it flies at over 620 miles per hour. The hump at the front of the aircraft holds the flight deck where the pilots and navigator sit and an upstairs lounge.

People have always dreamed about flying like the birds. But it was not until 1903 that someone first managed to fly in a machine worked by its own power.

Lighter than Air
Long before this, people had been up in the air in balloons. In fact, the first trip in a balloon took place as long ago as 1783. In that year two Frenchmen, the Montgolfier brothers, built a balloon that flew by hot air. They built a fire under it and filled the bag with hot air. Hot air rises — so the balloon rose too. Nowadays people still fly hot air balloons for fun.

Balloons have also been filled with hydrogen. Hydrogen is the lightest of all gases, so these balloons rose too.

But balloons could not be steered. They went where the wind took them.

The First Flights
During the 1800s many men tried to build aircraft that really worked. They knew that a kite would stay in the air. They made gliders that could carry a person. They tried steam engines, but they were too heavy. Many were nearly successful. But it was the Wright brothers who made the first powered flight at Kitty Hawk, North Carolina, in 1903.

The Wright Brothers
It was the gasoline engine that made the flying machine possible. The brothers Wilbur and Orville Wright learned about flying by building gliders. After hundreds of flights in their gliders they began work on their first *Flyer*. Into it they put a gasoline engine they had made themselves. The engine was attached to two pusher propellers by bicycle chains. On December 17, 1903, Orville flew the *Flyer* for 121 feet and landed safely. The Air Age had begun.

What Keeps it Up?
Why does an aircraft which is heavier than air stay up? It stays up because the aircraft's wings are a special shape. They are curved on top and flat at the bottom. As the wing rushes through the air, the air passing over the top has further to go than the air at the bottom. The air at the top goes faster, and when air goes fast there is less pressure. If there is less pressure at the top of the wing than at the bottom, the wing is lifted. The aircraft flies.

Before an aircraft can fly, the wings must be traveling fast enough to give sufficient *lift*.

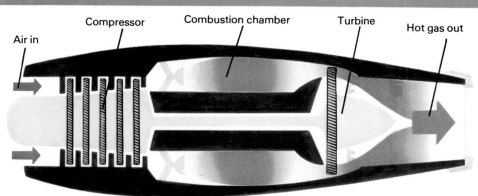

Air in   Compressor   Combustion chamber   Turbine   Hot gas out

The Jet Engine

Jet engines are quite simple. When air is shot backwards at high speed, whatever the air comes from is pushed forward. Blow up a balloon and let it go. The air rushes out and the balloon flies in the opposite direction.

A jet engine has a *compressor*, a *combustion chamber*, and a *turbine*. Air is sucked in at the front and squeezed tightly in the compressor. It is pushed into the combustion chamber and mixed with fuel (usually paraffin). This mixture burns fiercely and makes a stream of hot gas. The hot gas passes through the blades of a turbine. The turbine spins and drives the compressor. Then the hot gas rushes out at the back. This backward rush pushes the plane forward in the opposite direction.

Most planes nowadays have jet engines. But many still have propellers. These may have two, three, or four blades. There are even planes with two sets of propellers, one behind the other. Then, each set of propellers goes round in the opposite direction.

Wing Shape

Before the jet age, most planes had wings that stuck out straight on either side. But as the speed of planes increased, wings became more swept back. Swept-back wings make the plane more streamlined. There is less drag, less friction, at high speed. But straight out wings are better for taking off and landing. They give better lift.

The Swing-wing

In some planes the shape of the wing can be changed while the plane is flying. This is called the swing-wing. The bottom picture on the left shows the wing as the plane takes off. The center picture shows the wing going back after take-off. In the top picture the plane is flying at full speed.

Helicopters

Helicopters do not need runways. They can hover in the air or fly up and down — even backwards. But they cannot fly very fast. The helicopter has a rotor on top. The blades of the rotor behave like ordinary wings when they turn. They lift the helicopter. They also make the aircraft go forward because the pilot can change the angle of the rotor blades. There is also a small propeller at the tail. This stops the helicopter from turning round and round when the main rotor turns.

The plane on the right is a jump-jet. Its engine has four nozzles. If the nozzles are turned down, the plane rises straight up in the air. Then the nozzles are turned backwards and the plane is an ordinary fast jet.

Fun With Science

In this book you have learned about the basic ideas of science. Now you can check some of them for yourself.

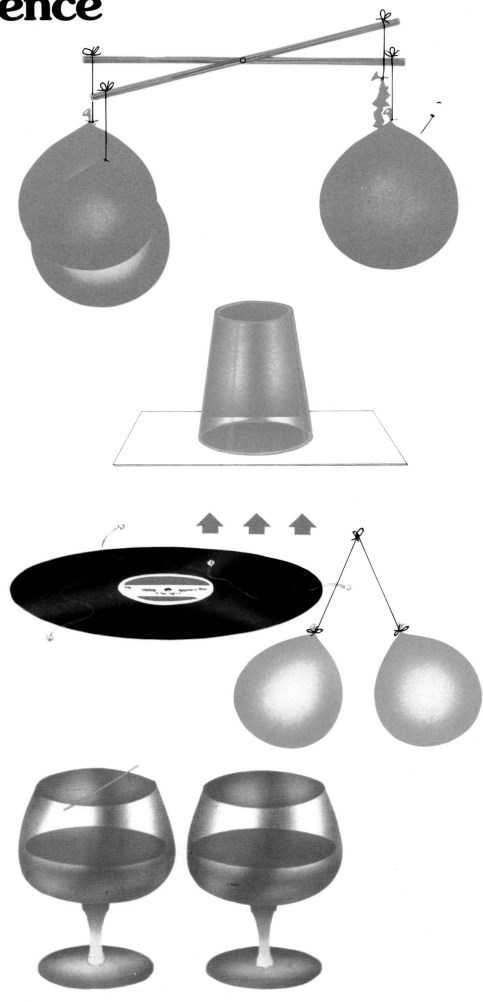

Air has Weight
Blow up two balloons and hang them at the ends of a stick that swings freely. Balance the balloons. If you then burst one of the balloons, the other will go down. The weight of the air in the full balloon pulls it down. Air has weight.

Air Presses in all Directions
Fill a glass with water and lay a piece of cardboard on top of it. Put a hand on the cardboard and turn the glass over. When you take your hand from the cardboard, it stays where it is and no water comes out. This shows that air presses up on the cardboard with more force than the weight of the water in the glass.

Jumping Balls
Rub an old record with something woolen. Put the record on a glass. Now drop some small balls made of rolled up aluminum foil on the record. When the balls come together they jump apart in a crazy way. When the record is rubbed it becomes electrified. The little balls become electrified too when they touch the record. As they have the same kind of electric charge they push each other apart.

You can show the same thing with two balloons. Blow up the balloons and let them hang together. Now rub both balloons on something woolen. They will push each other apart. Both balloons have taken electrons from the wool. They are both negatively charged. Two negative charges push each other apart.

Ringing Glasses
Take two wine glasses and half fill them with water. The glasses should be exactly the same. Place them close to each other, wet your finger and rub it slowly round the rim of one of the glasses. You will hear a ringing note from the glass. It has been made to vibrate by your finger. The vibration makes the ringing noise. Strangely enough, the second glass begins to vibrate too, although you haven't touched it. You can see this vibration if you place a very fine piece of wire across the top of it. The sound waves from the first glass hit the second glass and make it vibrate at the same speed. This will only work if both glasses make the same ringing tone when you rub your finger round them. If necessary, vary the amount of water in one glass until they both make the same sound when struck. They are tuned to each other — they are in *resonance*.

Magic Apples

Hang two apples about a half-inch apart. Blow between the apples and see what happens. They move closer together. Fast-moving air makes a lower air pressure. Blowing between the apples causes lower air pressure in the space. So the air on the other sides of the apples is able to push them together.

Hot Air in a Bottle

Drop a piece of burning paper into an empty milk bottle. When the paper has finished burning, stretch a piece of balloon rubber tightly across the mouth of the bottle. Soon the rubber is sucked into the bottle. The burning paper uses up some of the air in the bottle and heats it. This hot air expands. When the flame goes out, the air in the bottle cools and contracts. The air pressure outside the bottle is able to push the rubber into the neck.

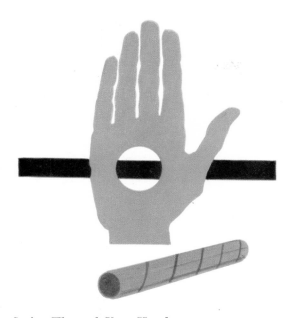

Seeing Through Your Hand

Look through a cardboard tube with your right eye. Hold your left hand up beside the tube. You see a neat hole right through your hand. We are used to both our eyes working together to tell us about the world about us. Here the right eye sees only the view through the tube. The left eye sees only the back of your hand. So the brain is confused by the signals it gets from the eyes. It does its best by making you think there is a hole in your hand.

Hit the Dot

Draw a dot on a piece of paper and try to hit the dot with the point of a pencil. You will find it quite easy. Now try to hit the dot with one eye closed. You will find it much more difficult. This is because we use both eyes to find the exact position of things. Each eye looks at the dot from a different position and tells your brain what it sees. The brain works out the exact position of the dot. With only one eye working, the brain finds its task very difficult.

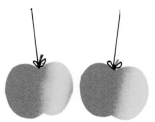

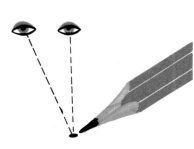

Powerful Air

Push a glass sideways into a basin of water. Then turn the glass round under water until its mouth is downwards. Now pull the glass almost out of the water as in the picture above. The glass stays full of water. This happens because the air pressing down on the surface of the water in the basin pushes the water up into the glass. This pressure is greater than the weight of the water in the glass.

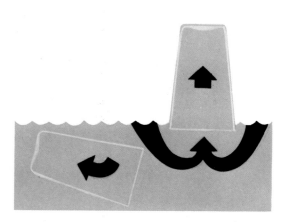

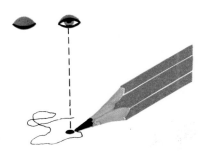

The Magic Spiral

Hot air rises. You can prove this by making a magic spiral. Draw a spiral on stiff paper and cut it out. Fix a needle in the end of a piece of wood or a pencil. Hold the pencil upright in a cork or thread spool and balance the spiral on the needle. If you place it on a radiator the spiral will spin round and round. The rising hot air is pushing on the paper strip and making it turn.

Index